George Stewart Hitchcock

The King of the Jews: A Poem

George Stewart Hitchcock

The King of the Jews: A Poem

ISBN/EAN: 9783743397644

Manufactured in Europe, USA, Canada, Australia, Japa

Cover: Foto ©Thomas Meinert / pixelio.de

Manufactured and distributed by brebook publishing software (www.brebook.com)

George Stewart Hitchcock

The King of the Jews: A Poem

THE KING OF THE JEWS.

A POEM BY

GEORGE STEWART HITCHCOCK.

Though this scroll describe triumphant evil,
  Yet the labour will not be in vain
If it spur some spirit to retrieval
  Of its treasure in despite of pain.
Arms are strong to guard and strike with vigour
  When the heart suspires with sympathy;
None the less this frail and lonely figure
  Tells of mightier means to victory.
True, a blow dismays the tyrant-coward
  And protects the weak from further ill,
But the strength to suffer is endowered
  With a life no tyranny can still.

Chatham:

Printed and Published by W. Hutchinson, 258, High Street.
1898.
[*All rights reserved.*]

CONTENTS.

The Inscription of the Poem. To Poetry.
The Greeting to Sorrow.
Scene 1.—A Fore-thought. The Valley of Tears.
Scene 2.—The Hill above Nazareth.
Scene 3.—The Wilderness of Judæa.
Scene 4.—The House of Simon, a Pharisee, at Capernaum.
Scene 5.—An Interlude. The Market-place of Shechem.
Scene 6.—The Court of the Women, in the Temple.
Scene 7.—The House of Joseph, the High-Priest.
Scene 8.—Before the Tower of Anthony.
Scene 9.—Calvary, looking towards the South.
Scene 10.—A Meditation. Calvary, looking towards the North.
Scene 11.—A Dream. The World of the Dead.
Scene 12.—An After-thought. Earth and Heaven.
The Welcome by Sorrow.
The Farewell to the Poem.

THE INSCRIPTION OF THE POEM.
TO POETRY.

Dim was the star when first it rose to bless
Night with a dream of purest happiness,
Trembling through tears and mists of wintry sighs,
But seemed a sun when mirrored in thine eyes;
And there I gazed until, immersed in thee,
My spirit found new founts of deity.

Success is grief, for mine the grim success
Of illustrating human feebleness
By this my tribute to the avatar
Of one small planet of a little star
Lost in the suns which form the Milky Way
And roll around the orb of greater day.

Though out of tune the lark and nightingale
Who sing within this tomb of shard and shale
Where rose and lily, wrought by artifice,
Shroud Grief in cerements of pulseless bliss,
Bear with my rhymes until my soul has wrought
A song divine in vigour, charm and thought.

Chatham,
 25th January, 1898.

THE GREETING TO SORROW.

Let me, unknown as the gift which I bring to thee,
    Rude as its riot of rhythms and rhymes,
Yet to thy throne ever lift, as I sing to thee,
    Songs of atonement for earlier times.

When thou didst palsy my mind and emaciate
    Body and spirit, I shrank from thy hold;
Since thou wert only a terror to satiate
    Blossoming manhood with famine and cold.

Faithlessness fettered and phantoms enfolded me,
    Babes which thy shadow had borne to Despair;
These are the means with the which thou hast moulded me,
    Branding my brow with the bruises of Care.

Mortals behold thee as gloomy and sinister;
    Yet I will trust thee, and come with belief
That I may find thee an angel and minister
    Nursing our souls with the virtue of grief.

Pity and pardon the altar I raise to thee;
    All of my hopes went to furnish its fires;
Even the incense ascending in haze to thee
    Came of a life's disappointed desires.

Tarry a moment, nor deem me importunate;
    Linger a little and look in mine eyes
While I proclaim thee as fairest and fortunate,
    Vision of God in a devil's disguise.

SCENE I.—A Fore-thought.

THE VALLEY OF TEARS.

(WHILE the winds, as they whisper, are hushing
  The care-wakened cries
Of all creatures, the Morning is blushing
  In fairest surprise
Where the dawn of the sunlight is flushing
  The grey of the skies.

Yet the glen is in gloom, for its gladness
  Has tasted the tears
Of the men, who are doomed to the madness
  Of hoping through fears
And sustain in their sorrow and sadness
  The yoke of the years.

But above, where the greensward is growing
  Distinct to the sight,
Stands a woman, resplendent and glowing
  As Angel of Light;
And a greybeard, enshrouded, is shewing
  As Angel of Night.)

THE ANGEL OF NIGHT.

Ages past beheld my sway :
  Ages yet shall bow to me,
Long as Night can hold at bay
  Light and Life and Liberty.

THE HUMAN CHORUS.

We, in darkness, deep and drear,
   Fettered, breathing only sighs,
All in vain our altars rear
   To the unregarding skies.

What avails a mortal's birth ?
   All for naught his toiling life ;
Seeing darkness fills the earth,
   And the world is torn with strife.

All we have we offer thee, [*To the Angel of Night.*
   Victims slain with sacred rite :
Hear but once our litany ;
   In thy pity grant us light.

THE ANGEL OF LIGHT.

See, in the times of the past,
   Life, in the slime of its youth,
Climbing and gaining at last
   Glimpses of beauty and truth.

There is the pathway of God -
   Out of the lifeless inane,
Path which the Spirit has trod,
   Mantled in passion and pain.

Now shall the singers and seers
   Breathe as the Spirit impels,
Weaving of terrors and tears
   Braids for the brows where he dwells.

THE ANGEL OF NIGHT.

Where the stars in their stations resemble
      The gems in a lyre,
There's a sparkle of raylets which tremble
      In semblance of fire.

'Tis a crown, which is glowing and seeming
      As mystic as morn,
But as pallid as palsy and gleaming
      With spikelets of thorn.

So the wreath, which is twined for the master
    Of music or verse,
Is a splendour but binding the faster
    His brows with a curse.

THE ANGEL OF LIGHT.

Deep in the soul, where no thinking or feeling
    Ever proclaims the defeat of the will,
Nature is living and moving, revealing
    Realms where no evil is able to kill,
Where, in the silence, her faith is appealing
    Mutely for freedom her life to fulfil.

God, who is wrapt in the shews of creation,
    Answers the wish of the thought-mantled soul,
Hushes to peace all its wild consternation,
    Points to himself as its fulness and goal,
Leading it out of its sad isolation
    Into the life and the joy of the whole.

THE ANGEL OF NIGHT.

Speak not to me of a Spirit transcending
    Aught that our senses can handle and see,
Glassed by the mirror, where mortals contending,
    Fitfully striving, are feigning to be.

THE ANGEL OF LIGHT.

Ages and ages have passed since began
    Sternest of struggles with life-slaying wrong;
Now that the ages have issued in man,
    Kingdoms of light are triumphant with song.

THE ANGEL OF NIGHT.

See how manhood trembles at my frown;
    And his the power to shake my throne!
Crowned he is, in truth, and what the crown?
    He knows the meaning of his groan.

Other creatures droop, and pass away,
    And never know how sad their state:
He, endowed with reason's ruthless ray,
    Must watch the working of his fate.

THE ANGEL OF LIGHT.

When piteous pain and plaint depress,
  And anguish shakes the feeble frame,
Then reason, think you, must distress,
  Displaying darkness by its flame.

But mind can, like a god, create
  From all the good that life can give
Of rapture, pure and passionate,
  A world of light where love may live.

Now, angel-brother, see the day
  Approach at last, when grief-born dreams
Create the light that ends thy sway
  And conquers darkness with its beams.

THE ANGEL OF NIGHT.

Let the day of man begin.
I will weave the web of sin
All around him and within.
Error reigns within his heart;
Madness flames about his brain;
And the powers of life depart
In an agony of pain.

THE ANGEL OF LIGHT.

While I am leading him
Upward, and speeding him
  On to defiance,
Thou art enslaving him,
Blinding, depraving him,
  Urging compliance.

Yet does the world-soul,
Planet-like whirled, roll
  On to perfection:
All of its movements,
Failures, improvements,
  Have this direction.

See how the starry ways
Seem like a starry maze,
  Lacking a single aim;

> Yet do those suns sublime
> Ever ascend, and climb
>   Nearer the central flame.

THE ANGEL OF NIGHT.

Look not to Nature for thoughts which will cheer
  Hearts that are withered and hopes that decay;
Blindly she struggles in hunger and fear,
  Starved in the past and thought-angered to-day.

THE ANGEL OF LIGHT.

To-day—the fruit of countless ages waging
  A war in which all pains and deaths were rife,
Which knew no dream of coming good assuaging
  The pangs of fierce and universal strife—
Is prophet of another day, presaging
  The grander scenes of yet a grander life.

Then nobler powers in mortal minds shall waken,
  And rend the veil which wraps the World and Man,
And, true to truth, by faithless fears unshaken,
  Shall reach at length a knowledge of the plan
Whose aim inspired the pains which God has taken
  In moulding life since Time and Space began.

THE ANGEL OF NIGHT.

Poor dwellers on this dying globe
  Which rolls along its changeless course!
Why should they feign a splendid robe
  To clothe the play of fate and force?

What can a mesh of quivering nerves
  Discover in the shews of sense?
And fancy's fleeting smile but serves
  To mock the man with vain pretence.

THE ANGEL OF LIGHT.

The mind of man can pierce the pall of sense.

THE ANGEL OF NIGHT.

To view his end, and tremble in suspense.

THE ANGEL OF LIGHT.

Hercules stands in the skies,
   Goal for the race of the sun;
Hercules, mighty and wise,
   Shines in the splendour he won.

Manhood, immortal, a star,
   Glows on the bosom of years,
Gleams in the distance afar,
   Crowned with its toil and its tears.

THE ANGEL OF NIGHT.

Poor planet, rent with rage and racked with pain,
Ere men attain that goal thy life shall wane,
And I shall chant this dirge to bless thy bane.

Dead, dead, and growing cold as yonder moon
Which told thy fate, when thou wast at thy noon,
Nor dreamed that death could still thy strife so soon.

Not thus thy life began on that great morn
When clouds of fire condensed and thou wast born,
For now the sun has shrunk from thee in scorn.

No breezes breathe a fragrance o'er thy lands;
Nor ocean seethes and roars around thy strands;
No dawn or sunset fires the vapour-brands.

What tongue could tell the tale of all thy years,
Or weave in words its web of hopes and fears,
And loves and hates, and joys and silent tears?

Thou grave of lifeless forms which throbbed in light!
Become a moon to breathe a baleful blight;
And warn the dawning worlds of coming night.

THE ANGEL OF LIGHT.

Earth may grow cold, and be a graveyard whirled
   In sleep and silence through the smiling skies;
The visioned beauty of a poet's world
   Is born in every breast and never dies.

Fair is the dream which Death and deathless Truth
   Have vested in a robe of sparkling tears,
Charming as Hope, and generous as Youth
   Inspired by noblest deeds of vanished years.

THE ANGEL OF NIGHT.

Come, Death, in ghostly gloom resume thy reign ;
For all created things are doomed to wane,
And mortal forms enfold the poet's thought,
The painter's dream and murmured music fraught
With mysteries. Yea, all of foul or fair
Shall reach thy realm through failure and despair.
Thine was the world ere life began to be,
When all from painful consciousness were free.
   Again the night of nothingness is nigh ;
   And life which vexed thy sleep with dreams shall die;
For thine the kingdom of eternity.

THE ANGEL OF LIGHT.

Come, Death, for laughing life shall break thy chain,
And spurn thy grasp to live in light again.
In pity come, for thou hast ever brought
The nobler life which moody mortals sought
In lonely gloom or in ambition's glare,
Where live alone the fumes of fear and care.
Come, Death of Selfishness, appear to me
In lightnings of heroic ecstasy,
   With softened splendours flashing from thine eye,
   Like those which speak of dawn in sunset sky,
Or those which crown a mother's memory.

THE HUMAN CHORUS.

The madness playing round a mortal's brain
Illumines Hope who vaunts herself Death's bane,
Robing her trembling limbs in radiance caught
From visions which the mocking rainbow wrought.
Her features, false as life, are wont to wear
A look composed of peace and lowly prayer.
But when pursued, she turns as if to flee,
With many a backward glance of grinning glee ;
   And to our wail of woe and fainting sigh
   Answers with mirth, as she floats slowly by
On poet-painted mists of melody.

THE ANGEL OF NIGHT.

Self-tortured minds, what need have ye to feign
The form of Hope and dreams of her disdain ?

Death is the good, and as a victor fought
With Life to win a truce for men distraught.
Death is the true, and be it mine to share
The wreath of ice which binds her ashen hair
Death is the beautiful, the poetry
Of calm and everlasting harmony.
   Throned in her placid loneliness on high,
    She feels no pain, hears no discordant cry ;
And starless night shall form her canopy.

THE ANGEL OF LIGHT.

O Love, divinest Love, thy life has lain
Too long enlapped in poverty and pain ;
For Death and Night in concert crush to naught
The world thy pangs and sacrifices bought.
Thine are the consecrated lips which bear
The voice of God ; and loving words prepare
The earth to don thy gentle panoply.
But where Death holds her court usurpingly,
   Thy royal strength shall rise at last to vie
    With her, and rend the foe who dares defy
The might of Love's eternal monarchy.

THE HUMAN CHORUS.

The powers, which move the world, in sorrow met
   To weave a royal wreath for deathless Death.
They seized the falling stars of night, and set
   Their splendours in a woman's dying breath,
And draped the diadem in mist as vague
As maiden's dream ere scathed by passion's plague.

The moody Night designed her ghostly veils
   Of frozen dews and clouds of sombre tone,
Which trembled like the songs of nightingales,
   And floated o'er the fire-flies in her zone ;
While baneful breezes breathed a blast and blight
To bless the gift designed by moody Night.

But Love, sweet Love, who lingered last, bestowed
   On Death the coronation robe of hope,
Which bore for ornaments a poet's ode
   And endless chains of pulsing hearts that grope
In darkest ways, pursuing and pursued,
While Life performs her little interlude.

SCENE 2.—The Hill above Nazareth.

(Lo! the sun with his dying splendours
   Empurples the sky and sea,
And to Carmel alone surrenders
   His grandeur and majesty.

'Mid the shadows of eve appearing,
   Stands Jesus upon the crown
Of the hill which is darkly rearing
   Its front o'er his native town.

And Jesus is standing, and gazes
   Where Nazareth sleeping lies,
But turns as he prays and upraises
   His brow to the sunset skies).

JESUS.

Moulder of sunlight and stars,
   Father of flowers of the field,
Moving where mist never mars
   Virtue, unveiled and revealed.

Hear me, and bend from thy throne;
   Hear, for I call unto thee;
Hear, for my cry is a groan,
   Sad as the moan of the sea.

Utter one word by my voice;
   Kindle my heart with thy fire:
God, in thy soul to rejoice!
   Once in thy breath to respire!

THE CHILDREN OF NAZARETH.

(Entering with JOHN, *and singing.)*

Under our feet
   The flow'rets are springing;
Voices, as sweet
   As Heaven, are singing.

Passes the daylight :
  The flow'rets are sleeping ;
Songs by the grey light
  Are changed into weeping.

Soon will the light
  Awake by its splendour
Flowers, the most bright,
  And songs, the most tender.

JOHN, *a young man.*

Look, his fierce and livid frown
  Darkens into mystery,
Like the vapours in his crown.

JESUS.

Speak, and tell me what you see.

JOHN, *pointing to the sun.*

There a dragon clothed in clouds
  Fills a flagon full of flame,
While the cirrus serfs in crowds
  Bow and tremble at his name.

Yonder lie his labyrinths
  Formed of foam and frosted flowers,
Where a hail of hyacinths
  Falls in slow and listless showers.

And the Moon, a mystic maid,
  Looks and leans in lovely light
O'er a beryl balustrade
  Towards her saviour, starry Night.

'Neath a roof of coral boughs,
  Gemmed with spinel stalactites,
Breathing beauties bind her brows,
  Born of pearls and chrysolites.

Deep the dragon drinks the draught,
  For he feels his vigour fail ;
Takes a sunbeam, aims the shaft
  At the moonlight, pale and frail.

Swifter than the voice of God,
   Speeds the sunbeam in its flight,
Fierce as faith and fair as fraud,
   Flying famished for the fight.

Now the noiseless Night is near,
   Leaps to save her satellite,
Blights the beam in full career,
   And asserts the reign of Night.

JESUS.

Guileless spirits, taught of God,
   Know the songs of buds and birds;
Find in cloud and flow'ry sod
   Poems and incarnate words.

JOHN.

Jesus, darkness comes apace;
   Wilt thou not return with us?

JESUS.

No; I wait to watch and trace
   Twilight's triumph tremulous.

JOHN.

Dost thou love the misty moon
   And the dreams which drape the night?

JESUS.

Yes; but they shall wither soon
   In the dawning of the light.

THE CHILDREN, *singing*.

   Soon will the light
     Awake by its splendour
   Flowers, the most bright,
     And songs, the most tender.

                   (*They go out with* JOHN.)

JESUS, *to Judas who enters*.

Peace to thee; why dost thou wander away
   From the town as the shadows of darkness impend?
Stay at my house till the breaking of day,
   And we'll tend thee and speed thee with love, as a friend.

JUDAS, *son of Simon the Assassin.*

No rest. No rest. The chains still bind
  The people I have sworn to free ;
While wealth and royal favour blind
  The Jew to loss of liberty.

No rest, until the people's might
  Has hurled the tyrant from his seat,
Until the God of our delight
  Has flung our foes beneath our feet.

JESUS.

Fear to utter rebel thought
  Against the power which rules us still.
Thou hast known the evil wrought
  On those who dared withstand its will.

JUDAS.

Ah, would'st thou betray me ? Then curses assail thee,
Nor ever the prayer of the righteous avail thee ;
But lost in the grave and unknown be thy story,
While ever the brave is enthroned in his glory.

JESUS.

Betray thee ? No ; the traitor's mind
  Is born in rage or wild despair ;
And fated so it may but find
  The scorn of age and childhood's stare.
But stay this night till morn arise
And day-dawn light adorn the skies.

JUDAS.

No rest for me ; 'tis the night of the nation.
  The people are sleeping, regardless of fame.
No rest till, roused from their humiliation,
  The people are weeping their loss and their shame.

(He goes out.)

JESUS.

Forth he goes, with the light on his brow
  Of a spirit illumed and consumed
    With the flame of a cause,
Such a cause as alone can endow
    With the highest applause,
Self-applause of a spirit self-doomed.

JESUS, *to Mary, his mother, as she enters.*

How brilliant is the roseate veil God throws
   Upon the features of the failing day ;
And oft I watch it thus, till fancy glows
   With dreams of worlds which never fade away.

Here, when my toil is ended, I can lie
   And quite forget my weariness, and dream
Of God, whose love appears in earth and sky
   And lights the world with sunset's radiant beam.

For, like a father in his faithful care,
   He watches over me, and still I hear
His voice in thrilling music, clear and rare,
   While love proclaims the death of feeble fear.

Perhaps, who knows ? and yet I hope, and dare
   To think that God will speak to men by me,
That by my words and works he will prepare
   The souls of men to claim their liberty.

Of old he spoke to them by those who felt
   The throes of higher life within and bore
His impress—those, in whom his wisdom dwelt
   And made them sons of God for evermore.

MARY.

   Child of my maiden joy,
  My only care and dearest treasure,
  Thy hopes recall the youthful pleasure
   Felt in my baby boy.

   Child of my maiden grief,
  I felt thy head in anguish throbbing :
  I heard thy voice in sorrow sobbing,
   Sorrow beyond relief.

JESUS.

Thus thy joy and sorrow alternating,
   Thou didst see my life as sad or pleasant,
With the angels round my pathway waiting
   And the future pictured in the present,
Dwelling now on life's loud song of gladness,
Now upon its undertone of sadness.

MARY.

Simple joy and simple sorrow
   Mark alone the poor man's fate;
Like to-day will be to-morrow;
   We must still endure and wait.

But the hands of dreams new-fashion
   This poor life composed of pains,
And create a purer passion
   Than the fire in earthly veins.

JESUS.

The lowly life which laughed in light,
   Or darkened in the dreary day,
Has still in silent sleep the sight
   Of God alway.

As fields, like these, which foamed in fight,
   Or echoed to the laughing crowds,
Or swooned beneath abysmal night
   And dismal clouds,

May know, in uneventful years,
   The passion of that patient Power
Which smiles in light or rains in tears
   To feast a flower.

MARY.

In the golden grey of eve,
   When crimson clouds have gone,
Ere the silver stars relieve
   The darkness creeping on,
Sadness stills the soul to sleep
   In dreams of peace to be,
Memories o'erwell and steep
   The mind in melody.

JESUS.

So sleeps the land, a star in sable set,
Like pallid patience pillowed on regret.

MARY.

The land is now a desolation :
   All the woes the prophets uttered,
   All the curses foemen muttered,
Are fallen now upon the nation.

JESUS.

There are realms the tyrant cannot enter :
   There's the kingdom of the soul,
Where is found no fierce and foul tormentor
   When the powers of God control.

And of this are mortals ever dreaming,
   Burning with ecstatic glow ;
Of all hopes which nerve their life-long scheming,
   This the noblest they can know.

Not ambition wakes their aspiration
   With such strength as this their dream :
Little value earthly wealth or station,
   When compared with this, they deem.

Who shall point to men the true direction
   How to realise their plan,
Kindle flames of love for God, affection
   And a fiery zeal for man ?

I shall go ; my spirit strongly urges,
   And my dreams with force impel :
I shall go where human passion surges,
   Where the floods of action swell.

I shall go ; let joy, or pain, or sorrow
   Wait about the path I tread :
Night may come, and gloom, but on the morrow
   Sunshine fills the world o'erhead.

MARY.

Jesus, hear thy mother's pleading ;
   Leave me not in loneliness :
Life is cruel, never heeding
   Cries of pain or deep distress.

Fear has seized me, lest, when needing
  All my sympathy and care,
Lest, when thou art wounded, bleeding,
  Not one comforter be there.

JESUS.

When fearful heart would seek a reason
  And a motive for delay,
Then valiant soul must count it treason
  From the battlefield to stay.

O God, regard my salutation ;
  Loved by thee, I fear not loss.

MARY.

Ah, so men stand in supplication :
  So are fastened to a cross.

SCENE 3.—The Wilderness of Judæa.

(FAR from toil and tumult of crowded cities,
   Two men stand where Jordan, the sacred river,
Pales with stars, those symbols of countless pities
   Weak to deliver.

Draped with dreams, the darkened and lonely regions
   Seem a camp of angels whose wings environ
Both the men with mightier power than legions
   Armoured in iron.

At their feet before them a youth is lying,
   Swathed in pensive pallor which stars are flinging
O'er the world, and pours his full heart of sighing
   Into his singing.)

      JOHN, *chanting as in a dream.*

Though the moonlight be misty and pallid,
   It reveals the sad face of the sea
By whose lips, as we listen, a ballad
   Is chanted in wave-tones for me;
And the clouds take the forms of the faces
   Which lightened in life in the strain
Of my music, though moodiness traces
   Sad runes in their wrinkles of pain.

O'er the wilds of the waters a glimmer
   Of gladness, more grievous than grief,
Is appearing, but death-like and dimmer
   Than eyes which despair of relief;
And the froth, that is born of the fretting
   Of tides and the sleep of the land,
Is grown grey as the grass in begetting
   A foam-wreath to circle the sand.

Roses pine in the weird light; their petals
   Are wan as they wither and fall
On the flint-stones, on thorn-bush and nettles;
   And woodbine grows hateful as gall;
For the rhyme and the revel of measures
   Which leapt from my lips in the light
Are bereft of my voice, and their pleasures
   Are numbed in the nursing of Night.

JUDAS.

Where is the flame which once fired to endurance?
   Chilled is my heart at the core.
Where is the hope which was sure as assurance?
   Stilled, like my youth, evermore.

Lonely and living thus listless in langour
   And powerless for patience or pride,
Lacking the fever of faith or of anger,
   I die, for my day-dreams have died.

JOSEPH, *a rich man.*

The high-strung soul, that strains its powers
   To reach a nobler life,
Will know in solitary hours
   The gloom which follows strife.

Then weary thoughts depress the heart,
   And fever frets the brain;
Till all the manly aims depart,
   And dreary dreams remain.

JUDAS.

I have no dream to madden and restore me,
   No strength to strain in strife;
For I am doomed to give to her who bore me
   A wasted life.

JOSEPH.

Why would'st thou daunt thy soul with idle terror
   And falter in thy fears?
Look where there shine through mists of sin and error
   Thy mother's tears.

JUDAS.

My mother's tears still whisper through the years
With power to calm my spirit, faint with fears,
   When memories of infancy, united
     With frenzied passions and ambitions blighted,
Awake my truer self which still reveres
My mother's tears.

And when I joined the ranks of pioneers
Who fought too close with sin which scathes and sears,
   My heart of hearts, though hardened, never slighted
My mother's tears.

Like one, bewildered and distraught, who steers
O'er faithless seas or sails on wind-swept meres,
   I pass my life in storms and toils, affrighted ;
     But yet a light appears to me benighted,
Which, kindled in her faded eyes, endears
My mother's tears.

JOSEPH.

   Weep for sins of youthful folly,
     Sloth and languor :
   Blush for moods of melancholy,
     Care and anger.

   Leave the weeping and the blushing :
     Face the morrow,
   Lest the past prevail in crushing
     Life with sorrow.

JOHN.

Each of them whirls in an orbit of madness,
   And circles some dream which attracts to its blaze,
Clad in a spirit of gladness or sadness
   As robed in its radiance or reft of its rays.

JOSEPH, *to Judas.*

Light is the laughter of the lark at noon,
   Rippling upon the tones of nightingales ;
Yet sad as Memory the mournful tune
   Born in the bosom of a flower that pales,
Although the sunlight bathe it from above,
Forlorn and famished for the lack of love.

Rich are the rain-drops sparkling in the grass,
    For in their smiles all splendours seem to meet;
Though weighed with woe the weary winds that pass
    O'er golden flowers which bloom among the wheat,
And moan that boon of beauty ne'er succeeds
In warding off the fate of worthless weeds.

Good as the God of goodness are the eyes
    Where infant innocence is sentinel;
But lurid lightning lingers in the skies
    Of those who held with sin and leagued with hell,
To whom the Past's impassioned quest bequeathes
A tomb of Hope adorned with rotten wreaths.

Immortal mortal, must the mood of earth
    Be mingled of such elements as these,
A chalice filled with mad, unmeasured mirth
    And pain of heart that nothing can appease?
Then thine be action's cup, whose vapour forms
The cloud of strife and strides athwart the storms.

        JOHN, *chanting*.

    Magic music moulds of mirth
        Temple-dome and fairy shrine,
    Where the passion-songs of earth
        Rise around a Void divine.

    Fairest faces fill the halls,
        Watching shapeless shadows spin
    Veils of light to blazon walls
        Twined of gold and hyaline.

    On a crystal floor and plinth
        Waves each pillared gossamer,
    In whose web of hyacinth
        Dwells a sleepless chorister.

    Clouds of snowy fancies curl
        O'er the beams of ruby rays;
    And the roofs of sunlit pearl
        Quiver in the mists of praise.

JOSEPH.

We seek to brace the faith that faints,
    To cheer the mind which onward gropes,
To voice the deep and dumb complaints
    Of broken hearts and blighted hopes.

We seek to sing the stronger strain
    Which wakes the manhood of the will,
And fires its efforts to attain
    That fame which falsehood fails to kill.

We seek to plant the thought which dares
    To live a lonely life of tears
In scorn and scathe, but buds and bears
    The noblest fruit of future years.

JOHN.

I would lie amid lilies and roses,
    Full-fed on what dreams have amassed;
Or I'd watch, while the water that flows is
    Arrayed in a mist and cuirassed
    With the brilliance the ripples have glassed
For the veiling of tears and distresses,
    When nature is gilded and brassed
In the warmth of the summer's caresses.

I would sleep in the day-dream that dozes
    Afar from the turmoils which blast
The slumbering peace that reposes
    In visions unveiling the vast
    And impalpable pure Protoplast,
Where never annoyance suppresses
    The fancies of spirits held fast
In the warmth of the summer's caresses.

For the blossom that poetry grows is
    More pallid than stars which contrast
With the gold that the lotus discloses
    To streamlets o'ergrown and engrassed;
    And the spirit which hurries aghast
From the struggle of worldlings confesses
    That the glories of strife are surpassed
In the warmth of the summer's caresses.

O wind, when my mind would forecast
All that thou in futurity hast,
  Reply with your whispers of yeses
That all will be well at the last
  In the warmth of the summer's caresses.

JOSEPH.

In the mystic morn of Youth
Beauty wore the robe of Truth,
And each fancy seemed a gem
Sparkling in her diadem.

Where her vestal footsteps fell,
Earth grew fair with asphodel,
In whose whispers poets heard
God's supreme and final word.

Manhood tore her robe apart,
Drained the blood at Beauty's heart,
Swearing that her robe should be
Wrought of Strength and Liberty.

By her throne, on either hand,
Rage and Wrong, his vassals, stand,
Waving in the wind their flags
Formed of Beauty's robe in rags.

And to weave her royal dress
Misery and Sordidness
Bring their famished slaves to spin
Raiment rich with tears and sin.

Ere the light of day is fled,
Beauty lies among the dead;
While, of metaphysic clouds,
Palsied Passion shapes her shrouds.

Now, in vain, we seek a trace
In the world of Beauty's grace;
But, above her lifeless heart,
Age erects a tomb of Art.

Oft some faint and feeble Faith
Steals a glimpse of Beauty's wraith
In the night of gloom and ruth,
And her robes are rags of Truth.

JOHN, *chanting*.

In the sky beyond the West
Twilight wrought the dead sun's vest,
Weaving clouds of purple mist
Into robes of amethyst.

Then the loving Seraphim
Sang sweet Sorrow's saddest hymn,
Till the echoes of the sphere
Murmured o'er the dead sun's bier.

All night long the stars bewail
Hush of song and loss of veil
Which had soothed a world undone
In the dying of the sun.

Day shall mould of golden mist
Vestments for its eucharist,
While the woods and rivulets
Chant an anthem of regrets.

Song and robe shall wrap the Night
Kneeling as an acolyte,
When the Morning stands as priest
On the mountains of the East.

JOSEPH.

When the dawn of the sunlight is breaking
  In twilight of falsehood and scorn,
And a truth in its trouble is waking,
  We herald the morn.

Unappalled by the passion and pallor
  Of fury and fear which are born
In the birth of all virtue and valour,
  We herald the morn.

Undeterred by the sceptre and sabre,
  And crowned with the spikelets of thorn
Which are wreathed for the forehead of labour,
  We herald the morn.

JUDAS.

To us has come a message,
  Fiery but tremulous,
Which bears a braver presage
  To us.

The hosts of ancient rebels
  Are ours, and ours the ghosts
Of deeds whose memory trebles
  The hosts.

JOHN.

To war with the world you require
  The wealth of a State or a Throne ;
And where are the men you'd inspire
  With strength that is strong as your own ?

JUDAS.

The reckless and men who have found
  The results of their labour destroyed,
The slaves of the mill and the ground
  And the hosts of the starved unemployed,
The victims of fraudulent schemes,
  And the youths who can never attain
The prizes which gleam in the dreams
  Of a noble and vigorous brain.

JOHN.

They will not strive for common weal
  But common home and common purse ;
And by your word you will appeal
  From curse unto a deeper curse.

JOSEPH.

In truth, some wild, fantastic hopes
  Are borne upon the storm of change,
Like spectres mocking him who gropes
  In worlds where all is new and strange.

But Nature's tread is slow and sure,
  And tramples down the weeds of night,
And suffers nothing to endure
  But that which springs from seeds of right.

JOHN.

Yes ; at the birth of it
  Visions are splendid :
What is the worth of it
  When it is ended ?

JOSEPH.

The single stream is forced to seek the ocean ;
  And single stars must own the sway of all ;
For self avails alone for self-devotion,
  And freedom's proudest crown is won as thrall.

But see, the selfishness of former ages,
  When earth was but a theatre of strife,
Still clings to these, the later, nobler stages
  Of progress toward the goal of fuller life.

For still we offer human sacrifices,
  And worship self with heaps of human dead,
Our sisters, slain by foul and loathsome vices,
  Our brothers, slain by toil and want of bread.

Yet even now my heart is rapt, beholding
  The glory of the future, juster time
When Man becomes the faith of men, enfolding
  The castes and creeds of every race and clime.

Then thrones and empires find their consummation
  In one great State of undisputed sway ;
And all the world becomes a single nation
  Which treads in unity its upward way.

JUDAS.

Service, Equality, Brotherhood, phrases
  And speeches that die in the day of their birth,
Measure the might of the man who appraises
  In leisure and pleasure the sorrows of earth.

Nakedness, hunger and thirst are the real
  And menace us, keeping our bodies in thrall,
Blighting the fancy which feigns an ideal
  Of Truth and of Hope and of Justice for all.

Truth has no charm where Necessity shivers
   In hovels apart from the glances of God,
Dwelling in darkness by ice-covered rivers
   Of tears which no smile of the sun ever thawed.

Hope cannot lighten the life that is blasted,
   And has but created a shadowy throne
Gilded with splendours, which Rage has contrasted
   With all of the sorrow the spirit has known.

Justice alone is our prayer and petition;
   And Justice alone is the cry of the soul.
Would you refuse it? Then crime and sedition
   Shall stalk through the land and o'erpower all control.

JOSEPH.

There is a life new-born in death's dark hour
   And folded in the arms of dreamy Night,
Like that which sleeps within the autumn flower
   And wakes in spring to bathe in streams of light.

And though to you our age may seem to wear
   The mantle of decay, it holds the seeds
Of self-abandoned men whose bosoms bear
   The flowers of simple truth and noble deeds.

JUDAS.

The people still are prey of feud and faction;
   The nation still a slave to selfishness;
The heirs of time are born in noble action
   And moulded by a youth of strife and stress.

And they, the destined chieftains who inherit
   A heart to feel and brain to plan success,
Shall grow with swelling times and rule by merit
   Of arms to save and truthful lips to bless.

JOHN, THE BAPTIST, *entering*.

O Israël, what mighty voices
   Proclaim the advent of thy king;
For Heaven smiles, and Earth rejoices
   With all the transports of the Spring.

This year, the fields, untilled and idle,
  Are with the world in deep accord,
And wait the meeting and the bridal
  Of Israël and God the Lord.

The land, in robes of nature's weaving,
  Is looking for Messiah's light
That comes, restoring and retrieving
  The losses of the lengthened night.

And on the spirit of the nation
  Descends the comfort Heaven gives
Through Heaven's ancient proclamation,
  Behold the One Eternal lives.

The kingdom of our God is speeding
  To harvest as the Lord revealed ;
And he himself directs the weeding
  Of fire-doomed darnel from his field.

Make clear across the fenceless spaces
  A pathway for Eternal Right ;
And level in the sterile places
  A terrace for resistless Might.

JUDAS.

Then move the heart of God who gave
  Reward to wrong.   His wealth has sealed
The forehead of the soulless knave
  Who sins in joining field to field.

THE BAPTIST.

Nay ; for Eternal God proclaims
  By all our popular unrest
His scorn of low and selfish aims
  And zealous love for those oppressed.

JOSEPH, *to Judas.*

Why should you rave at the riches around you,
  And grumble and groan till the brave interfere ?
Why should you wail for the wealth which has bound you
  And held you as captives for many a year ?
For your own weakness and folly have crowned you
  With fear.

Have you no heart but for hate and suspicion ;
  No lips but for lisping of liberty's name ?
Blind are your eyes to the worth of the vision
  The spirit of man is unfolding in flame :
Aye ; and your flags are but rags of derision
  And shame.

JOHN.

They say that you are weak and feeble men
  Impelled to sudden speech by sudden thought,
Like those who hold the poet's fiery pen
  And fashion frenzied nothing out of naught.

JUDAS.

They say ! They say, as they have ever said,
  And spread the solemn lie or mocking tale
Which flames about the living and the dead
  Until their sunny glories fade and pale.

Who fears the slander wafted by a breath ;
  And who would therefore fling away his cause
While Virtue can prevail o'er scorn and death
  To bless the brow which sought but her applause ?

JOSEPH, *to the Baptist.*

Help us, brother, yours as ours the battle,
  Yours as ours the worldling's snarls and sneers,
Grief and labour, till the harsh death-rattle
  Crowns with rest the fret of fevered years.

Join us, brother, in our friendless season,
  While our eyes are scalded with their tears,
While our faith in man is counted treason,
  While the people spurn their pioneers.

Brother, see the world of woe and sorrow
  And the many held in rich men's thrall ;
Watch with us the dawning of the morrow
  Bright with health and happiness for all.

Ours are not mere selfish mean devices
  Planned to spread a creed or party-name :
Ours the truth that grows by sacrifices ;
  Others' wealth accomplished by our shame.

Brother, comrade, heed the voice within you ;
  Do not league you with the stronger part ;
Come with us, for ours the cause to win you
  Ill repute and toil and peace of heart.

THE BAPTIST.

A prophet's word is not in clamour,
  But moves in music as a bird
When gentle spring-time tries to stammer
  A prophet's word.

Replete with love, its tones enamour
  The faint who fear for hope deferred,
Nor win the world with worthless glamour.

But he who wields it as a rammer
  Shall leave impressions, dull and blurred ;
Lightly must fall that holy hammer,
  A prophet's word.

JOHN, *chanting as in a dream.*

Oh, give heed to the true thoughts which hallow
  My song, lest it sink in regret,
Looking less on the feeble and callow
  Expressions in which it is set.
Could I chant in the strain of a poet
  Whose music is strange or antique,
Would your heart listen longer, or show it
  Responds by the crimson-hued cheek ?

Who can fathom the feeling which fashions
  Life's robe ere 'tis rended by death,
Or persuade to a patience the passions
  That cease but in ceasing of breath ?
Though our world be so tearful and thornful
  Yet thou mayest plant, unaware,
The grief that upgrows from a scornful
  Rejection, whose fruit is despair.

Love is lord of the night and the daytime,
  Enthroned in all dreaming as king ;
And his mood is as wayward as Maytime
  That's mad with the raptures of Spring.

And thy glances are gemmed with the jewel
   All-potent to charm from the fire
Of the sun-world a flame for the fuel
   Of longing in which I suspire.

Thou, who charmest all ills and disasters
   And bringest good issues from wrong,
Be propitious to poor poetasters,
   Thou spirit of music and song;
For each feeling and thought is a facet
   That sparkles in Poetry's rays,
And the temper contemns a mere tacit
   Confession of faith and of praise.

JOSEPH.

Yes; Art may feign and fashion forms
   Of Truth and Beauty linked by Love,
But Nature's face is rent with storms
   And hopeless as those stars above.

JUDAS.

Where are the songs of olden days
   Which roused the manhood of the soul
To deeds that won the nation's praise,
   And fettered fears that would control?

Where are the songs of olden days
   Which echoed like a thunder-roll,
And rang throughout the endless ways
   That wander from the starry pole?

THE BAPTIST.

The lyre is broken and the music fled
   Thither whence melodies have no returning,
For each renounces life to weave instead
   A symphony surpassing man's discerning.

The higher tones are new-born wails of earth:
   The stronger strain is wrought of ripe endeavour;
And its deep undersong is made of mirth
   Which pulses through the spheres of God for ever.

Its choral majesties are moved and surge
    Against the rocks where Time sits, gaunt and hoary ;
And with a stern, resistless passion urge
    The swift unveiling of eternal glory,
When earth shall hear the harmony and swell
    With rapture moulded by the miracle.

JUDAS.

And now when we grow faint and falter,
    A million screechings shout our shame ;
Dumb is the spirit of the psalter
    That once could kindle souls of flame.

THE BAPTIST.

Through the wastes of the star-lighted waves
    And out of the harbour of Night,
Sails a ship with a cargo of slaves
    Who shiver in terror and fright.

Then the winds, in that passion of spite
    Which roars like a coward and raves,
Tell the sailors that forces of might
    Have fashioned their watery graves.

And the laughter of losels and knaves
    Is merry in mocking their plight ;
But their souls are of manhood which braves
    The darkness that curtains the light.

JUDAS.

The ship is Israël ; the sailors,
    The prophets who have led the race
Of Abraham in spite of railers
    To see the light of Moses' face.

THE BAPTIST.

Not kinship with the patriarch
    Availed for Isaac, but the ram ;
For God can call from sunless dark
    Enlightened sons for Abraham.

JUDAS.

But Israël has been the Lord's vicegerent
  And witness of his Oneness to the world,
And o'er the nations, folly-led and errant,
  The banner of his holiness unfurled.

Must we regard our serfdom as the pittance
  Rewarding us for sacrifice and hymn?
Does such return assure him an acquittance
  From recompense to faithful Seraphim?

Better by far have bowed to Bel or Rimmon,
  For they could crown their worshippers with wealth;
But we must weep and wail like helpless women,
  And even nurse our hopes in shameful stealth.

JOHN.

Then learn profounder lore,
  That so thou mayest gain
Thy soul, and evermore
  Live freed from hopeless pain.

There falls upon thy brow
  A ray of light divine,
For heaven opens now
  And all its wealth is thine.

And yonder I discern
  Fair forms of purest light,
Which blaze until they burn
  To naught the power of sight.

But seek not wealth nor those,
  The spirits of the blest,
For farther scenes disclose
  Supreme content and rest.

Thee, Beauty, thee alone,
  We seek by paths untrod,
To share thy crown and throne
  As one in soul with God.

This is our one desire
  To pass from earth and sense
To where thy inmost fire
  Consumes with heat intense.

JUDAS.

Thou fool, this is a dream,
  And thou art mocking me
With formless shews which seem,
  And only seem, to be.

THE BAPTIST.

Vainly, for ever vainly, fancy searches
  For treasure hid beyond the reach of sense;
Worse than in vain, for all her efforts purchase
  A doom of spiritual pestilence.

Vainly she boasts her faith to be implicit
  And deems her skill surpassingly adroit;
For in her folly she but treads illicit
  And treacherous paths to silliest exploit.

Here in the actual find the God-wrought balance
  Of life which weighs the worth of good and sin,
And proves less sensitive to myriad talents
  Than to just deeds and stern self-discipline;
While death stands by to seize with cruel claws
The lighter fruits unsunned by duty's laws.

JOHN.

But, priest and prophet, dost thou not remember
  The poet's theme of sacrificial lives?
Or hast thou never known the dying ember
  Bear visionary flamelet which survives?
So death avails to burst the bond of nature
  And set the spirit free
From frenzied mood and passion's usurpature
  To live in liberty.

  For what is death but rest
  From labours which invest
One moment in perfervid folly?
  And life is the supreme
  Quintessence of a dream
And insubstantial melancholy.

Death is for me a mute and mystic symbol
    Which veils and yet reveals the spheres of truth,
And is unknown to sense however nimble
    And confident with earth-born fire of youth.
Dead to the world in fact, or e'en in fancy,
    Freed from its sordidness,
I roam those realms which toil and necromancy
    Dimly perceive by guess.

    And there nor right nor wrong
    Disturbs the reign of song;
No drab and stiffened dress of duty
    Compels the symmetry
    And synchromy to flee
The dream of everlasting beauty.

JUDAS.

    Lonely my lot;
      Pity its pain;
    God is forgot;
      Branded the brain;
    Knowledge is not;
      Vision is vain.

JOSEPH, to *John*.

Frail poet, many a blast of evil parches
    The brave advancing over human bones;
And thou would'st be companion of their marches
    With songs unmeaning as that night-bird's tones.

JOHN, to *the nightingale*.

Voice of the night, whose tones of plaintive sobbing
    Painlessly swathe the heart in sweet regret,
Art thou bereaved, or dost thou chant the throbbing
    Of thrilling passion in thy canzonet?

Longing to learn the lonely song of sorrow
    That swells with lavish loveliness of grief,
Feeblest of poets, I would die to borrow
    Thy throat while moonlight trembles on a leaf.

Why dost thou linger in this land, belated
  And lost to all thy lady-loves who roam
In flowery isles which western waves created
  To be for aye the songster's springtide home ?

Dost thou remain to succour me in spelling
  The meaning of thy mournful melodies ?
Yes ; for at last I understand thee, telling
  Eternal woes and world-wide agonies.

      JESUS, *who has entered*.

If thou dost recognise the spirit springing
  To self-expression in the song-bird's tone,
Tell us the word which it persists in singing
  Through changing moods as various as thine own.

      JOHN, *as in a dream*.

My throat with impetuous throbs
  Is trembling and shaken, and thrilled
With murmurs and musical sobs,
  And soars into song ere 'tis stilled.

The plainings are never complete,
  But quiver and shiver, and break
In cries like the shrieks of defeat
  When dream-fettered spirits awake.

In light none has leisure to learn
  Of battles which harrow the heart ;
And worldlings are weak to discern
  The worth of my passionate art.

But greed and ambition take flight
  When Eternity flows from the stars,
And darkness alone has delight
  In music which selfishness mars.

My complaint and my pleasure are twin
  And born of the breezes and streams
For my body is reptile within ;
  My spirit is fashioned of dreams.

I long not for beautiful form
  Or prizes of strength or of skill,
But pant for a peace in the storm
  Which I have no virtue to still.

At times I attain to the tones
   Which move in the music of mirth
Till broken with shrillness through groans
   Heard hoarse from the grief-laden earth.

Do visions avail for a bird
   To purchase a life out of death,
Or shall I be lost as a word
   Is lost in the lulling of breath?

JUDAS.

Does not the heart grow full to bursting
   When manhood masques as feminine
And mumbles numbers, while we're thirsting
   To drink one drop of freedom's wine.

And naught but falsehood ever grew in
   The soil which pining fancy feigns
Amid the nation's mass of ruin
   Beswept by fiercest hurricanes.

JOSEPH.

One half thy song has sense and reason,
   And wert thou satisfied to sing
Of poverty discrowned by treason,
   We'd crown thee as a poet-king.

THE BAPTIST.

Or if thy tones were ripe with teaching
   And nerved mankind to fetter crime,
What influence was thine and reaching
   Through long neglect to endless time!

JESUS.

Beauty is born in patience or in pining,
   In moods of languor or in lighter mirth,
While poets weave its opal pall, entwining
   The myriad pulses of the panting earth.

And life is given in the song's emotion,
   Invigorating heart and brain and limbs,
Kindling the world with rapturous devotion
   And love surpassing e'en the Seraphim's.

Sing as thou wilt, the spirit which inspires thee
  Creates an archetype by which we mete
Our movement upward ; and the flame which fires thee
  Forbids the faithless from a foul retreat ;
And God who gave the gift of song to thee
Shall vindicate the voice of poetry.

JUDAS.

Who art thou ; and what seekest thou to-night ?

JESUS.

Jesus ; and come to share the Baptist's rite.

THE BAPTIST.

'Tis rather mine to be baptized of thee.

JESUS.

Nay ; grant my prayer, for so it needs must be.

JOHN.

For so thou would'st absorb God's word in all.

THE BAPTIST, *to Jesus*.

Then follow me, as David followed Saul.

(They two go out.)

JOHN, *chanting*.

Within a thornset dell
  A child lay down to rest :
A faded floweret fell,
  She dreamed, upon her breast.

She wept ; the flower was pleased,
  And woke to life and smiled ;
And straight a longing seized
  The spirit of the child.

She rose, and sought the flower
  Which came to her in dream ;
But found it not in bower,
  Or field, or silver stream.

But, while she searched in vain,
  It drooped within the eyes
Of those who pine in pain
  For one to sympathise.

JUDAS.
Why change thy madness for weak sentiments?
JOSEPH.
Or dost thou wake from dreams to sober sense?
JOHN.
I played with pleasure, shaped of the shivering
Of star-lit treasure, borne on the quivering
  Of leaves at leisure from the terror
  Wasting the world with the winds of error.
The moody madness wronged in caressing me,
Unnerved with sadness life in repressing me
  Thus held from gladness : till a duty,
  Blest in its gift to me, shewed new beauty.

JESUS, *to the Baptist, as they return.*

  Farewell, farewell, for God impels
    My soul to seek the wilderness;
  And ere I go where darkness dwells,
  Farewell; farewell, for God impels
  My life to paths which terror tells
    Are painful paths of dire distress.
  Farewell, farewell, for God impels
    My soul to seek the wilderness.

THE BAPTIST.

  Farewell, a darksome world of dirges
    Is fashioned by a miracle,
  And from its inmost heart emerges
    " Farewell."

  The force of blindfold nature surges,
    And in its shock is heard a knell,
  Announcing that our path diverges.

  But lo, the world is scarred by scourges
    And holden fast in hatred's spell;
  Then go, for love of mortals urges
    Farewell.

JOSEPH.
Art mad, to turn from man to solitude?

JUDAS.
He seeks the hermit's visions which delude.

THE BAPTIST.
There God will visit undistracted hearts.

JOHN, *as Jesus goes out.*
Nay; Jesus, stay. O God, the light departs.
(He falls in a faint.)

JUDAS.
So fast, so fast,
   A life has flown,
And all is past
   Ere aught is known.

One word is spelt;
   One thought has thrilled;
One fear is felt;
   And all is stilled.

JOSEPH.
No grief, though death has taken
   An early sheaf;
And though our breasts be shaken,
   No grief.

He sleeps within the star-land,
   Nor laughs, nor weeps,
But, crowned with peace for garland,
   He sleeps.

The night grows full of faces
   We loved in light;
And soon our day embraces
   The night.

Till then our faith shall quicken
   The minds of men,
Nor shall we faint or sicken
   Till then.

And song shall shrine our glory,
   And love prolong
Our lives in tearless story
   And song.

THE BAPTIST.

Stand not in idle meditation;
   Death has not sealed his countenance;
His heart regains its true pulsation,
   And he awakens from his trance.

JOHN, *wildly*.

The Spirit rapt me in a miracle
   That so the Tempter might display his wiles;
And see! the grey inhabitants of hell
   Are seeking to pollute me with their smiles.

The purple phantoms of the baneful stars
   Fly through the dampness floating in the dark;
And moonbeams mock me, grinning through their bars
   In pallid gleams, impassive, cold and stark.

God hides his face from me, his chosen one,
   And bids his angels leave me to my hour;
For I was born to be his word, his son,
   The last expression of his love and power.

But look, my legions come from every clime,
   The souls I quickened with the life of song,
The fairy fancies robed in rhythmic rhyme
   And worlds redeemed from wretchedness and wrong.

The fiends grow faint, and offer me their world
   If I will worship falsehood, strength and lust;
But at my word the worthless gift is whirled
   To death's domain and pounded into dust.

My world, resplendent in its silver mist,
   Is throned for ever in an azure haze,
Chanting to God the perfect eucharist
   And thrilling him with everlasting praise.

The devils fly, and God can breathe in peace,
   For I establish thus his ancient plan;
But I must travail yet, till my decease
   Has won the God in men to worship Man.

They bound my arms, reviled me in their scorn;
   And now they wait to see me sacrificed:
They wreathe my burning brow with bitter thorn.
   Behold, I am the son of God, the Christ.

SCENE 4.—The House of Simon, a pharisee, at Capernaum.

(THE sunlight falls on the brilliant hues
　Of robes which are worn by the crowd
Who throng the court and discuss the news
　In tones that are eager and loud.

And there it seems as if woe released
　Her victims, the poor and distressed,
To view the scene of the morning feast
　Which Simon prepares for his guest.

His friends recline on the cushions around
　A table which, painted in red,
Is raised a foot from the carpeted ground;
　And Simon is set at the head.

And next him Jesus is lying, and sees
　A woman, well-known in the street,
Who weeps while, crouching and bowed on her knees,
　She washes the dust from his feet.

With tears removing the dust and the soil,
　And drying his feet with her hairs,
She breaks the casket of spikenard and oil
　Which hangs from the necklace she wears.)

THOMAS.

May never a dream of ambition invite
My soul to adventure a dangerous flight,
To burden itself with contrition and care,
An object of malice and envious stare.

But never the absence of spirit deprave
My life to the state of a down-trodden slave,
Whose heart does not heave with the loathing of life
Nor seeks an escape by the noose or the knife.

I'd live in the twilight of place and of truth,
And, casting away all the dreams of my youth,
Abide in contentment, nor ever would feel
The pride of position or raging of zeal.

SIMON, *one of the Assassins.*

I'd feel the surging rage and scorn
Of breasts in which rebellion's born,
Where Freedom's fearless frenzies warn
   The world of light
That mocks the murky mists of morn
   And ends the night.

JOHN.

I would be great with a greatness surpassing the fame which expires
  On the lips of humanity,
Paying no heed to the voice of the world, though it shout till it tires
  In its feverish vanity ;
Ever to stand, like an angel, regardless of men, whether gazing
  Admiring, or sneeringly ;
Hear but the voices of eloquent silence, nor blaming nor praising,
  But chanting endearingly :

Sleep, sleep in sweet and undisturbed repose,
  For now thou hast attained thy rest :
No more thy wearied heart is stung, or knows
  The fears which once profaned thy breast.
Sleep, sleep, the thunders roar, and tempests rage,
  And storm-cries shriek, and whirlwinds fill
The scene, which thou didst tread in pilgrimage,
  Until it will, like thee, be still.

SIMON, *called the Rock.*

And so, would'st thou in death forget
  The world with all its stress and strife,
Nor pay thy debt with one regret
  For ills besetting human life ?

But griefs, although, 'tis said, they break
    The gentle heart in which they make
Their far-from-gentle home, yet wake
    The soul to live for honour's sake.

The noble instincts, hopes that lead
    A man to wait a nobler doom
Than for a while to rot and feed
    The worms which breed within the tomb,

Are surely rays divine, and stray
    From light that makes eternal day;
Not fatal gleams, like those which play
    On marshy ground and lead astray
    The traveller on his midnight way.

THOMAS.

In the hushing of music and laughter,
    In silence which sobers the brave,
We may wonder what waits for us after
    The march to the grave.

We may long for a life that is deathless
    And strong in a surer resource
Than the body which, bloodless and breathless,
    Is flung from the course.

It will spur on the soul to endeavour,
    Fulfilling the yearnings of youth;
And we'll live in the lie, for we'll never
    Awake in the truth.

SIMON, *the Rock.*

There are feelings unrecorded,
    Fancies never framed in speech,
Deeds of valour unrewarded,
    Aims a mortal cannot reach.

Are these born to fume and dwindle,
    Like the foam which crowns a wave,
Or to fire the brain and kindle
    Hopes of life beyond the grave?

THOMAS.

So fancy feigns a splendour in the clouds
   Which fevered thought suspends o'er dying souls ;
As suns in setting gild their fleecy shrouds
   To crown themselves with mimic aureoles.

SIMON, *the Rock*.

But when thou would'st arrange in ordered thought
   The myriad sights and sounds surprising thee,
Then thy philosophy dissolves in naught
   Unless the good revive in worlds to be.

THOMAS.

I spin no speculative scheme of Nature,
   Explaining all the universe of Fact ;
Nor fling a plummet, wrought of nomenclature,
   In boundless and eternal tides of Act.

What power have I to bind with bare idea
   The diverse forms which multiply until
The world is crowded and no panacea
   For want appears except the leave to kill ?

Nor dare I claim to know of an here-after
   For us when ears are deaf and eyes grow dim ;
Nor would I choose excessive tears or laughter,
   Or yield my reason for a poet's whim.

SIMON, *the Rock*.

All await the rending of the veiling
   Which conceals the life that follows this ;
And amid their effort and their failing
   Look up thitherward for endless bliss.

THOMAS.

Earth has squalor, and the Heavens splendour ;
   Earth has fever, and the Heavens calm ;
Yet what man is eager to surrender
   Earth's most smarting wound for Heaven's balm ?

Can it be we think a bold profession
    Stills the storms of fears when thought-lit glooms
Pass across the soul in swift succession,
    Shattering its temples and its tombs?

We persuade our fellows to denial
    Of the fact before their eyes and ours;
And with candles falsify the dial
    When the shadow speaks of fleeting hours.

Night shall come in spite of all our striving,
    Nature mocking all the hopes we feign;
Nor lament that there is no surviving
    This poor life for mortals tired of pain.

SIMON, *one of the Assassins.*

If hymns adorning death
Should be but perfumed breath
    To soothe the sense,
Or torch's falsest flare
Which by its ghastly glare
    Makes dark more dense,

Why lose our lives in vain,
Nor gird our loins to gain
    A Heaven here?
For wrath still rules in wrong,
And scorns the righteous song
    Of saint and seer.

JOHN.

And would you satisfy my full ambition?
    Then make perpetual music in my heart;
Endow my brain with poet's intuition;
    And drape my dreams in all the hues of art.

Give me to understand what Nature stutters
    Through all her moods and in her million tones;
And tell me all that mirth or madness mutters,
    With all that peace resigns and patience owns.

Charm me with faith that knows not change or rancour;
   Give me a memory unsoiled by shame;
Show me a future where my soul at anchor
   Rides royally on sunlit seas of fame.
Yet I would sacrifice these gifts to creep
Through dreams of mystery to peaceful sleep.

THOMAS.

We dream of Heaven till the falsehood stifles
   The sense of wrong and injury on earth,
Soothing our sorrows with a poet's trifles
   And with his madness murdering our mirth.

And lo, through all the scrolls of our long story,
   Chaos is monarch of the gloomy years,
For men bemocked their minds with royal glory
   Or Paradise restored in other spheres.

Let dreams persist to be a feigned oasis
   In life's Egyptian bondage for a maid;
But we are men, and build upon a basis
   Of Nature's force and reason unafraid,
That so the pyramid survive the spell
Which dreamers weave to make the earth a hell.

JUDAS.

We need a voice whose tones shall sway
   All men and heal our sense of wrongs
With visions of a future day
   To which full recompense belongs.

JESUS.

I hear it in the whispers of the wind,
   In every sob and lisping of the stream,
In sadder notes which memory would bind
   To weave a music-mantle round a dream.

I hear it in the infant's wailing cry,
   In sighs which live in grief on woman's breath,
In gasps of men who would, yet dare not, die,
   But hope to find relief at last in death.

It speaks the earthly language of my heart,
    And throbs in love and anger, soft and wild;
It tells of earth, her storm-clouds rent apart,
    In smiles reflecting Heaven undefiled.

    JAMES, *brother of Simon the Assassin.*

        Hope is fleeting,
        Still retreating
          Into gloom,
        Where its glimmer,
        Growing dimmer,
        Lights the tomb.

    SIMON, *one of the Assassins.*

In the past there were torrents of trouble
    And floods of despair,
And each life disappeared as a bubble
    That burst in the air.

In the present the spirit is frightened
    With frenzy and gloom,
And the hopes are disheartened which brightened
    The dark of the tomb.

    JESUS.

O'er the darkness of woe and of weeping
    There flashes afar
From the future, wherein it is sleeping
    And dreaming, a star.

It is tearful and winged with the warning
    That day has withdrawn,
But returns in the spring of the morning
    To herald the dawn.

    JAMES, *brother of Simon the Assassin.*

But, if never a thought of the future impel
With the glories of heaven or horrors of hell,
Can a man be unmoved by the spectres that glare
'Mid the torture of fasting and struggle of prayer,
When the fiend strives to strangle his faith with his fears,
And his spirit is spent in a passion of tears?

THOMAS.

But why should we attempt to bear
The burden others' sins prepare,
And what can any man attain
In spending thus his heart and brain ?
For, while the hero lives, a yell
Of execration startles hell ;
But when, rejected, scorned, he dies,
We clothe his life in splendid lies,
And tell the legends o'er and o'er,
With prophecies which went before.

MATTHEW.

'Tis true the heart, that's good and brave,
   Is often by the rulers slain :
The people wake it from its grave
   To live in worship once again.

For those who sway the sword of state
   Can never view without distrust
The flinging wide of freedom's gate
   Or manhood rising from the dust.

But we, who pant from hour to hour
   With poor man's toil and poor man's grief,
Will turn to him who boasts of power
   To bring us justice and relief.

When once I served beneath the king,
   In Herod Antipas I sought
The Man of God whom psalmists sing ;
   But all my dreaming came to naught.

As each pretends the holy oil
   Has set him for the task apart,
We suffer hunger, pain and toil
   To follow him with eager heart.

But surely now our Jesus' word,
   Simple as truth and yet sublime
Is like a song in which is heard
   The message of a newer time.

JOHN.

I lit the years of youth
  With fancy's beam,
And touched the robe of truth
  In dream.

Then all of life was gold
  Without alloy,
A mine, with wealth untold
  Of joy.

Till, shadowed o'er with gloom,
  The life, so brief,
Became a living tomb
  Of grief.

But henceforth, undismayed,
  I'll wait, nor weep,
Until my life is laid
  To sleep.

PHILIP.

Fuming and fretting,
  Onward we travel,
Sobbing in setting
  Feet on the gravel.

Sharp are the splinters;
  Thorny the hedges;
Whirlwinds and winters
  Live on the ledges.

Chasm and stone-shower
  Wait for the brave band,
Sparing some lone flower,
  Mark of the grave-land.

Darkness grows deeper;
  Steeper the passes;
Brushwood and creeper
  Tangle with grasses.

Summits are shrouded;
  Moon-beams diminish;
Star-light is clouded:
  When shall we finish?

JOHN.

Why not leave the world of feud and faction,
    Watch in peace from far the forces surging?
See their reckless aim and restless action
    Ever to a single issue verging,
    All in naught or merest chaos merging.

See the Sphinx regarding all the ages
    With a glance untroubled by emotion:
See the god adored by eastern sages,
    Deaf to all his worshippers' devotion,
    Sleeps like sunlight on the tranquil ocean.

PHILIP.

Let your picture of patience be painted
    In hues of the rose,
For its faith never faltered or fainted
    In terror of snows.

Though it pales with the pallor of passion
    Its heart can unfold
All those founts of affection which fashion
    A treasure of gold.

It may blush as if dipt in the day-dawn
    And drest in a dream,
Or reflect back the pearl of the grey dawn
    As mantled in cream.

It is graced with the glory and splendour
    Of sea and of sun;
But it always is tearful and tender
    And deeply undone.

JESUS.

    Deep calls to deep;
        Loud is the chorus;
    Storm-torrents leap
        Madly before us.

    Tempests arise,
        Wild in their raging;
    Shrill are their cries,
        Ruin presaging.

Cloud-masses drift
  Onward in thunder;
Light-flashes rift
  Darkness asunder.

Fearless of fear,
  Calm in your wonder,
Listen and hear
  God in the thunder.

PHILIP.

But who is strong enough to cope
  With ills that o'er the world prevail?
The scheme in which we put our hope
  Can only bravely, nobly, fail.

Why should we wring our hearts, and grieve
  For multitudes of mournful mood?
Can human sympathy relieve
  The crowds who cry and faint for food?

JESUS.

Nay, my Philip, every human heart is beating,
  Ever swelling, ever growing
  With indwelling, grace-bestowing,
Powers of sympathy which, manhood's state completing,
Make a mortal more than mortal in his vigour,
  Seldom lending thought to pleasure,
  But expending all his treasure
In assuaging grief that rages in its rigour.

Now the effort seems but thrown away and wasted;
  And illusion, quickly dying,
  Leaves confusion, death-defying,
Far more grievous for the bliss which fled untasted;
But the kindly soil of human hearts will nourish
  And will cherish efforts slighted:
  Though they perish as if blighted,
Ages hence the seeds of noble deeds will flourish.

When the earth appears in cold and wintry beauty,
  Snows are winding round the mountain,
  Ice is binding fast the fountain,
And the chilling blast is killing love and duty;

But the earth profusely, in the spring-time, giving
    All the wealth of all her being,
    And the health of nature seeing,
Shares and wears the fair and rare delight of living.

A WOMAN WHO WAS A SINNER.

Rabbi Jesus, look on me:
On thy feet my scalding tears are falling;
In my heart are hateful fears appalling:
    Jesus, let me cling to thee.

When I lay, a helpless infant, sleeping,
    Borne upon my mother's breast,
Watch and guard the angel-hosts were keeping:
    God was smiling on my rest.

Soon the dawn that blest the child would
    Merge into the noon of day:
Passions fierce and feelings wild would
    Bend my life to pleasure's sway.

Then the bliss of loving and the gladness:
    Now the anguish, scorn and dread;
Now remorse and soul-consuming madness,
    Broken heart and fevered head.

SIMON, *a pharisee.*

Master, beware of that woman unholy:
    Look at her features engraven with sin
Vile and degraded, her body is solely
    House for the devils who riot within.

JESUS.

Once two poor men in distress
    Were fain to borrow:
One, too sanguine of success,
    Would pledge the morrow
For a loan of sums immense;
    But the second
Followed judgment and good sense,
    Duly reckoned
All his power to pay, and deemed
    Small loan the best.

Then they failed: in grief one seemed
    With dread opprest:
Not the other, for he dreamed
    Himself still blest.
Tell me now, if he who lent
    Would cease to sue,
Which would know, as freed he went,
    The love most true.

SIMON, *a pharisee.*

The greater love is doubtless shewn
By him who had the greater loan.

JESUS.

The lesser gift was given thee,
A form of law and prophets famed in olden story,
    A land which shall hereafter see
The Lord's Anointed reign in universal glory.

The greater gift of God was given
To her who kneels, and weeps, and cries aloud my name,
    A form once fair, a soul love-driven,
And light which flashes from her eyes in fiercest flame.

The law, as taught by thee,
    The lives of all oppresses:
She, in captivity
    To sin, her soul distresses.
Thy prophets' light, vanished in sadness:
Her hopes, once bright, banished in madness.

Now forgiveness, gently stealing
    O'er the tempest in her soul,
Pacifies her faith's appealing,
    Making shattered spirit whole.

Now her grateful heart is glowing
    With its life renewed in pain:
Now her life-stream, once more flowing
    Godwards, lives in love again.

  · No water didst thou place for me:
    She bathed my feet with tears.
No kiss have I received from thee:
    She kissed my feet, all fears.

No oil was poured upon my head:
   Anointed were my feet.
Arise, for all thy shame is fled:
   Returned is love more sweet.

THE WOMAN WHO WAS A SINNER.

O soul of love, thy words, enchaining
   My heart with hopeful love, reveal
The God who hears the lone complaining
   In blighted woman's mute appeal.

To follow thee, be this my mission,
   To serve in menial ministry,
To share thy toil, endure derision,
   And live in glad captivity.

MARY, *entering*.

Jesus, my son, return again with me,
   Nor trust the promise of deceitful dreams:
My soul is prey to dread anxiety
   And sees the issue of thy daring schemes.
Oh, rest content in poor, unknown estate;
   Nor seek the prophet's place, the prophet's fate.

JUDAS.

   Heed not the voice of despair.
What for the waste of a life can atone?
   Haste to the city, for there,
Waiting for thee, is a sceptre and throne.

   Crushed by the tread of the foe,
Prey of the nations, the people is grieved;
   Rise thou and strike a strong blow;
Show us the national glory retrieved.

SIMON, *a pharisee*.

Is this the man to mount Messiah's throne,
   Who talks, and tells some pretty fables?
A peasant, poor, unlearned and alone,
   A centre he of village babels.

JUDAS.

My father, Simon, loves to tell
   Of glories gleaming through the mists of morning:
   Around my heart he wove a spell
Of soul-absorbing dreams, of fierceness scorning
   All pains in hope to raise the race,
Our race that writhes in restless indecision,
   To cleanse again the Holy Place
And crown the whole with God in prophet-vision.
   The world awaits a mighty king,
And, peaceful, stands in silent expectation:
   Arise, and let the nation sing
Again the ancient Songs of Restoration.

JESUS.

Nay, my Judas, I would rather
   Raise again the kingdom in each breast,
Where the spirit of my Father
   Should be welcomed as the dearest guest.

See what broken hearts are lying
   In my path and fill the world with sighs;
See the veil of grief undying
   Laid in bitterness on dying eyes.

Yes; I rise to reign in splendour
   Such as earthly king has never known;
My sole sceptre, love most tender;
   And in grateful hearts my love-built throne.

JUDAS.

But thou wilt slay the nation's foemen
   And brand with shame each renegade
When David's throne fulfils the omen
   Which John the Baptist's word displayed.

For life is not of milk and honey,
   But lives in all that we abhor
Till Judah's sky grows calm and sunny
   And Chaos dies in Yahveh's war.

And while the women's hands dishevel
   Their hair, and while they weep and wail,
The men who dare outmatch the devil
   Find strength and wit of more avail.

JESUS.

If life is a battle and nature a chaos,
    Much sorrow is born of our efforts to frame
The kingdoms of earth that have strength to dismay us,
    Full-fed with our fear and enthroned in our shame.

Though nature be shaken with fiery upheaval,
    And wrinkled with traces of ice and of flood,
More fierce is the truce in the triumph of evil
    When earth is besmirched with the blackness of blood.

True peace and true war are the kingdom of heaven
    Where minds have no master save God the supreme,
Where gladness is multiplied seventy times seven,
    For dread disappears as a horrible dream.

The spirit who spurns the defects in the fortune
    Of want or of weakness which statesmen award
Grows blest in the Blest, nor desires to importune
    The Spirit it owns as its Father and Lord.

SCENE 5.—An Interlude.

The Market-place of Shechem.

(The children dance around the market-place
   And fill the town with laughter, light and gay,
   The while their coloured robes and pleasant play
Enrich the scene with joy and gentle grace.

The elders, seated by with solemn face,
   In slow dispute wear out the waning day;
   The younger men describe some village fray
And feats in mimic strife or doubtful race.

Behind are flat-roofed houses in array;
   Steep, barren cliffs; and, far above, we trace
The height of Gerizim in purple-grey,
   Whose rugged summit cleaves the azure space
Where clouds, in listless languor, slowly stray,
   Like frosted fleeces fringed with crimson lace.)

    ADAR, *a boy, entering and speaking to Asher.*

  Here are some flowers I gathered to-day:
    I brought them home for you.
  How, in their pride, they delight to display
    Their tints of white and blue.

  Here is the poppy that colours the fields
    With scarlet, rich and fine:
  Here is the gold which the apricot yields,
    Whose leaves, like silver, shine.

ASHER, *an old man.*

All these, my child, are beautiful to me,
   And linked in thought to days I'll see no more,
   When dreaming youth would paint the future o'er
With joys to come and glories yet to be.

But not in sadness does my memory cling
   To days long past, nor would I feel again
   The throb of passion or the thrilling pain
Of life that buds and blossoms in its spring.

The dreams of youth and thoughts of riper years
   Are mine ; and though the winter, wan and chill,
   May seize upon my heart, and, ruthless, kill,
I see beyond : again the spring appears.

But see, these flowers are sacrificed and give
   To us their fragrance, colour, form and glow
   To charm us for a moment, and bestow
In dying all their wealth on us who live.

And yet, not all their wealth, for that is less
   Since they are torn from life and power to grow :
   Alas, that selfishness can never know
How worlds of beauty, undesired, may bless.

ADAR.

   Thou art not grieved : I only thought
   To show my love for thee, and sought
   The fields where flowers appear most fair.

ASHER.

No ; children's love is to the lone
A light dispelling grief and care.

ADAR.

Had you no children of your own ?

ASHER.

Two little boys were mine to keep,
   And good little boys were they :
One of them loved to pine and weep ;
   The other one loved to play.

One of them wandered everywhere:
   Wherever he chanced to go,
Glancing around, he fancied there
   The symbols and signs of woe.

Then would the other view the earth,
   And smilingly turn to me,
Say that he saw the birth of mirth
   In glee of the land and sea.

Seeing the world as it appears
   When coloured by human eyes,
One of them saw a vale of tears;
   The other but cloudless skies.

Everyone blessed the sight of him
   Whose smile was as bright as day:
Seeing the tearful, eyes grew dim,
   And glances were turned away.

Two little boys are laid to sleep;
   However, the worlds they made
Linger while men shall laugh or weep
   And live in the light or shade.

ADAR.

And where do your little boys sleep?

ASHER.

In a grave, where a mantle of flowers
Is growing and long grasses creep
   To protect them from storm-winds and showers.

ADAR.

Who killed them?

ASHER.

              God, who ever wills the best,
Beheld their lives with love and gave them rest.

ADAR.

It was wicked of God: Yes; and when I am grown
   I will climb up the mountain, and where
He is living alone in the height, on his throne,
   I will meet him and fight with him there.

ASHER.

Nay; little Satan, believe that his will
 Is to girdle with goodness the earth:
When he appears to afflict or to kill,
 He is bringing new lives to the birth.

ABSALOM, *a young man, entering with Zadok.*

The Jew we found but yesterday,
Alone and faint upon the way,
Has passed from us. Our help no more
Avails to cure him and restore.
No more may Nabal boast his power:
His victim needs must curse the hour
He fell into his hands.

ZADOK, *an old man.*

                    Now wait
The white-robed angels at the gate
Of Heaven to free him from disease
And cleanse his soul from sin and doubt.

NABAL.

The only gate of Heaven he sees
Is that by which they drive him out.

ABSALOM.

Ah, thou art only wise to kill:
The sick are ever doomed to lose
Their lives to prove thy vaunted skill.

NABAL.

I practise only on the Jews.

SUSANNAH, *entering and singing.*

Rebecca discovered a stranger stand
 One eve by the fountain's side:
He came from a prince in a far-off land,
 Who sought her to be his bride.

Oh, when shall a messenger come to me
    With tidings like those to tell?
I'll follow him over the land and sea,
    Through death and the gates of hell.

THE OTHER MAIDENS, *also coming from the well.*

Here is our poet returning;
    And where has he tarried so long,
Leaving us lonely and yearning
    For tones of a love-breathing song?

ABSALOM.

What is song?
    A sigh in sable,
Or a wrong
    In folds of fable,
Or a chain
    Of art to tether
Love and pain
    And hope together.

SUSANNAH.

Song is fire
    Which prophets kindle,
In attire
    From poets' spindle;
Or a star
    Of truth and treasure,
Flaming far
    In light and pleasure.

ASHER.

A bard may view with half-closed eye
    The play of light on wood and stream
Till Heaven flash from out the sky
    In one supreme and subtle gleam.

But poets who have boldly trod
    The sad and painful paths of earth
Are priests and prophets of the God
    Who gave their work and knows their worth.

ELNATHAN, *entering.*

I wandered and roved through the groves where the silver streams glide
And watched how the waters would leap down the mountain's steep side
And felt, with the senses awakened, wherever I trod,
The breath of the breeze on my brow, like the breathing of God.

I heard in the stillness of morning the musical note
Which calls on the creatures of God, whether near or remote,
To join in the anthem of praise, which ascends, like the mist,
When Morn and the mountain have met in embraces and kissed,
Until, in the noonday, the anthem is loudest and swells
With tones as sonorous as roars of the ocean, and tells
Of passionate striving that dies, in its madness, away,
When eventide hushes to silence the chorus of day.

Then perfumes, unnumbered, arose from the herbage to fill
With exquisite sweetness the air of the valley and hill.
The winds wafted swiftly the sound of the magical word
Which, only by ear of a woman or poet, is heard;
And when it is mentioned a mantle of beauty and bliss
Envelopes the world, like the blush of a maiden's first kiss.
It thrills in the nightingale's song, in the coo of the dove,
In whispers of roses and lilies; its name—

THE MAIDENS.

It is love.

ELNATHAN, *to Susannah.*

Love that has not one single claim
   To be beloved in turn by thee,
But that it must remain the same
   Through sunshine and adversity,
   Controls my heart and motions me
To offer in despite of shame
Love that has not one single claim
   To be beloved in turn by thee.

The phantoms of a future fame
   Shudder, and faint, and cease to be;
And all my hopes prove halt and lame
   As they arise and crowd to see
Love that has not one single claim
   To be beloved in turn by thee.

SUSANNAH.

Why didst thou leave us,
Thou who art dearest
Of all that we own?
Why thus bereave us,
Poet, and grieve us,
Us, who receive you,
Ever believe you,
Us, whom thou cheerest,
The lives that are lone?

ELNATHAN.

I went to the mountains to hunt for a thought.

THE MAIDENS.

Then come, sir, and tell us what prey you have brought.

ELNATHAN.

I heard a brooklet sing one night,
  As it looked at the moon above:
Descend to me, my heart's delight,
  That my life may be lost in love.

The moon replied, and tossed her head:
  I am not for a waif like thee;
If I should condescend to wed,
  I would marry the deep blue sea.

The brooklet's smile grew still more sweet,
  As it shimmered and danced for glee
And said: I'll hasten on to meet
  My beloved in the deep blue sea.

The moon said naught, but shone more bright;
  And I looked at the brooklet's bed
And saw the moon, and knew that night
  That the moon and the brook were wed.

NABAL.

What tales these youngsters tell! I think he said
The moon and brook had power to speak and wed.
When I was young, some threescore years ago,
There was a poet here, whose verse would flow
More smooth; and he could tell a tale quite free
From foolish talk about the moon or sea.

ASHER.

Take heart, my poet, after many a year
Thy name shall mentioned be, and some child here
Shall crown thy memory with praise and say:
There lived a poet in my younger day.

ELNATHAN.

But praise is sweet to living ears,
 And I would have the earnest now
Of glories which the future years
 Shall wreathe about my lifeless brow.

SUSANNAH.

Why should'st thou care for it, seeing we love thee?
 All of us love thee: well ; all but me ;
And, like the mountain that rises above thee,
 Thine is the crown of eternity.

Though, like the mountain, thy forehead arises,
 Never adorned by a wreath of the earth ;
Yet 'tis thine eyes which the light first surprises
 When, in the morning, it comes to the birth.

Here is a garland of flowers as a token
 Thou art our prince in the kingdom of song
Where, as in dreamland, the silence is broken
 Only by love and the conquest of wrong.

Come, then, and sing for us ; sing to our dances :
 Thou wilt confess thee as more than repaid,
Fired by applause of the youth and the glances
 Flashing like swords from the eyes of each maid.

ELNATHAN.

What shall I sing ; or gay, or grave ;
Of life on land, or ocean wave ;
The brave man skilled to fight, nor fly ;
The love that wept, but could not die ?

SUSANNAH.

Surprise with skill prehensive
 Some beauty ere it dies,
To yield a more intensive
 Surprise.

Disclose the secret sobbing
   Within the blushing rose ;
And, that which soothes its throbbing,
   Disclose.

As tears oft shine prophetic
   Of fair and happy years,
Sing of lone love, pathetic
   As tears.

ELNATHAN.

Unmeasured splendour and unfathomed yearning
   Compose existence, yet are unexpressed ;
And myriad miracles are mute, returning
   To die unuttered in their mother-breast ;
Nor can a pang surpass my heart's, discerning
   How weak are words to answer its behest ;
For all things fade, nor can my feeble breath
Preserve one glory from the gloom of death.

The forms of beauty build a fairy palace
   Of pensive shades and tints of pallid blue,
Whose dome's the sun, and from his burnished chalice
   Is flowing light of every flaming hue,
Until our souls are lead and hearts grow callous
   Through watching wonders springing ever new ;
But were they keen as once, they could not give
Their thought a language that the thought might live.

The world's wild music holds my mind in tension,
   Or soothes it with a melody benign ;
Though oft the discords shatter thought's suspension
   And force my heart to feign an anodyne
Lest that my soul attain a new dimension
   To grow in grace and vigour more divine ;
And thus the anthem dies, nor may my art
Treasure one passage for my panting heart.

The universe of transient illusion,
   Wrought on the surface of deep floods of tears,
Withered by winds of fever and confusion
   And fretted by the limits of the years,
In hastening to an impotent conclusion
   When Death shall rule throughout the starless spheres,
Passing in pain, nor have I power to tell
The tale of earth that holds all heaven and hell.

Ah, could I seize one shadow as it passes,
   Or stay one rapture in the sunbeam's kiss,
Or learn one whisper of the leaves and grasses,
   My soul would revel in a realm of bliss,
And spurn the dark despair and doubt's morasses
   Which close our little life's parenthesis;
But all things flee, nor have I skill to stay
The blossom's blush which dies with dying day.

My chant is but an echo of the wailing
   That girds the world as with a ghastly zone,
The sigh of those whose brilliant youth is paling
   And passing to a sallow monotone,
Blended with tears of brave men sailing, sailing,
   O'er tides of toil toward tearless lands unknown,
And hymns of hope, whose melodies compete
With silence, symbol of a faith's defeat.

THE YOUNG MEN.

Sing us the song the foemen hears
   And straightway takes to flight.

THE MAIDENS.

Sing us a tale of love and tears,
   Of hope and pure delight.

THE OLD MEN.

Sing of the peace of him who nears
   The end of life's long night.

ALL.

Sing us a strain which is free from the fetters of art,
Swayed by the force of a passion that swells in the heart.

ELNATHAN.

There came a Jewish youth to meet a maid,
   A daughter of Samaria's hated race,
   And for their meeting chose a shaded place
Where olive branches o'er a fountain played.

He found her 'mid the gold and scarlet flowers
   Which seemed to form a moon-lit magic ring;
   Her raiment like the green of leaves in spring;
Her mantle darker, like the grass in showers.

Their hearts were heavy, sad and sore dismayed,
    For they must part, or he was forced to face
    The doom of ever infamous disgrace
Which brands a soldier, by his fears betrayed.

The Jewish priestly king, that John accurst,
    Had chosen him to march against this town
    And raze our Temple, glorious in renown :
So bade Hyrcanus, of our foes the worst.

She heard the tale in sorrow's silent spell ;
    Her bosom heaved, oppressed beneath its fears ;
    Then weeping sore, she steeped his breast in tears,
And, kissing him in silence, looked farewell.

He's gone, who was to her a god descending,
As heathens dream, upon the earth and blending
A mortal form of beauty past expressing
With God's own nature, earth and earth-men blessing.

He's gone, but still she stays and waits, delaying,
To watch the wistful, mournful shadows playing
About her features in the water clear ;
Until it seems as if sad tears appear
In mirrored eyes, and withered leaves enshroud
Her face till all is hidden by a cloud.

He's gone, and bears in heart and mind a treasured semblance,
Engraven in his life and set in sad remembrance,
Of her who shed a light of beauty, rich and tender ;
For so the floweret in its love-time will surrender
The riches of its perfume, that the scent may capture
A straying insect lost in dreams of love and rapture.

He's gone, but she is still his goal, the guide
Which leads him and will never be denied,
For him the never-setting, polar star
Which flames the centre of the worlds afar ;
And though a cloud conceal it for a day,
Or feeble mind to other object stray,
Yet this he knows, that phantom gloom will cease
And in her love he'll find the perfect peace.

    On Shechem's walls her warriors stand
        To watch the Jewish dogs advance :
    The sunlight falls upon the band,
        And gleams from helm and sword and lance.

In joy the earth awoke this morn
   To taste again the joy of life,
Without a cry or cloud to warn
   The peaceful world of coming strife.

But now, advancing to the fight,
   Behold the Jews, that race abhorred ;
And Shechem's sons prepare to smite
   The enemies of God the Lord.

The cries of passion, madness, rage ;
   The wounded writhing in their pain ;
The brute aroused in man to wage
   The deadly war of brutes again.

The old men, bowed in bootless prayer ;
   The wail of women, weird and wild ;
The young men battling with despair ;
   The blank dismay of maid and child.

Ah, God ; that deeds like these should be :
   The mothers see their infants slain ;
And youthful brides, while outraged, see
   Their husbands' dying look of pain.

The flames have seized upon the town,
   And cries of piteous grief and woe
Ascend to God and strive to drown
   The mirth of murderers below.

The Mount of Blessing is ablaze ;
   The Temple flames athwart the skies ;
And, where the people sang his praise,
   The Lord can hear their dying cries.

Where shall the lover find his maiden ?
   Will he not seek in the captive throng ?
What though she be with fetters laden,
   He will protect her from shame and wrong.

Would she were there, or where they're heaping
   Those who were breathing at break of day,
Where now the shades of eve are creeping
   Over the bodies of Murder's prey.

Not there she lies, 'mid heroes slain defending
Their faith and homes, to whom e'en death is lending
A glory in defeat and crowns their name
With deathless wreaths of honourable fame.

But see her corpse, disrobed, dishonoured, thrown
Among the maidens who, like her, have known
The fate of women in a captured place,
Whose hideous murder is their least disgrace.

The awful picture smote his reeling brain,
And rent his heart with rage and racking pain,
And broke life's golden goblet, scarcely tasted ;
While passion, in a ruby river, hasted
To find a spring within the dull, cold earth,
By which it might ascend and come to birth
Once more in rosy flames of fairest flowers
Arrayed with rich and ruddy hues in bowers
Where buds and blossoms bloom and blush while keeping
Their watch and ward o'er winsome maiden sleeping.

Then his faith and hope and youthful gladness
Vanished, swept away in storms of madness ;
And a scorching wind of fevered care
Seemed to blast his spirit with despair.

Voices which the lips of nature send in rapture to the skies
Were to him the weary weeping of a woe that never dies :
Nay ; the radiance of the sunshine and the brilliant pictures painted
On the azure of the heaven were defiled by death and tainted ;
For they told of passing beauty and of wonders that decay
When the nightfall robes in darkness all the splendours of the day.

Then the world of stars, so distant, in its solemn rhythmic motion
Spoke of gods as void of feeling as the heart of placid ocean,
Who appointed but one pathway for all creatures cursed with breath,
Leading them from love in dreamland to the slaughter-house of death.

  But once, as he lay in a dream-troubled sleep,
   The breath of the night-wind awoke him again ;
  And dread seemed to crush him and palsy to creep
   With chill from his limbs to his heart and his brain.

For, lo, in a vesture of silence and awe,
    And raising a forehead on which he could trace
The tale of a glorified sorrow, he saw
    His darling who shone with a love-lighted face.

Her eyes were as clear as a mountain-side spring,
    Reflecting the rays which the stars of the night
Had sent as the heralds of heaven to fling
    A glory around her and crown her with light.

Those lips, once as red as the blush of the flower
    The pomegranate bears, never quivered or stirred
As once in the days when her breathing had power
    To charm with a whisper or rule with a word.

But silent she stood with the gleam on her head
    Which shone with that paleness of silvery gold
The moon will display when she lies on a bed
    Of indistinct shadows, so grey and so cold.

He gazed, and endeavoured to break from the spell
    Which held him enchained with the silence of fear:
He struggled to speak, that once more he might tell
    The love he had cherished through many a year.

Then slowly the form of the figure grew faint
    Till, chilled to the soul, he beheld her depart;
And casting away all the bonds of restraint,
    He nourished with weeping the pain of his heart.

But when, like a tempest-tost sea, at the last
His spirit but heaved through the storm that was past,
He waited in peace for his death to unite
His life and her life in the regions of light.

THE MAIDENS.

'Tis sad that hate can rule our fate,
    And kill with grief and sadness
The love which strives to crown our lives
    And fill the world with gladness.

ZADOK.

'Tis sadder still to view the height
    Of Gerizim against the sky
And know that there, through Jewish spite,
    Our temple-courts in ruin lie.

No more with splendour, as befits
   Samaria's God, do we adore
Or fall before him where he sits
   Upon the mount for evermore.

THE YOUNG MEN.

But at last when the dawn of our triumph shall break,
Then the blood of the heroes, now silent, shall wake
With a song that shall answer the pleadings which rose
From the women and aged in the day of our foes;
For the sons of Samaria then shall unite
In the rage of inherited wrong to requite
All the woes we have suffered, the scorn we have borne;
And the friends of Jerusalem ever shall mourn.

ABSALOM.

Still love is the motive of song,
   The love of a man for a maid,
While duty and loathing of wrong
   Are lacking a voice unafraid.

ASHER.

Do not the flowers in darkness hide
   The toil of duty,
And crown their loves with all the pride
   And spoil of beauty?

ABSALOM.

But where is the beauty discerned
   In a time that is selfish and vain,
Which wails for reward never earned
   And in horror of labour and pain?

Each flames for himself and is hoarse
   In the praise of his self-nourished gleams,
Or dwells in his self-channeled course,
   Like the sluggish and slumbering streams.

ELNATHAN.

I have met it in meadow and mountain,
   In dreams of the past,
In the songs of the flower and the fountain;
   And found it englassed

In the gladness which flows from the smiling
    Aglow in the face
Of a mother or sister, beguiling
    A child with its grace ;
In the depths of the dreamlands that glimmer
    In eyes of a bride,
Where affection grows fonder, and dimmer
    The glances of pride ;
In the glory which crowns an ideal
    Of life at its best,
When it soars from the slough of the real
    Of strife and unrest.

ABSALOM.

Ah, life is but a being's bane,
    A weary waste of wilful folly,
A dreary dirge with dull refrain
    In chords of gloom and melancholy.

The rich man trembles for his wealth ;
    The poor man lives in schemes fomented
By secret clubs which plan in stealth
    A heaven for the discontented.

ELNATHAN, *to Susannah.*

The winds of the woodland, the streamlets in panting,
    The sunlight which sings till it sinks in the sea,
The stars of the midnight, for ever are chanting,
    Susannah, Susannah, Susannah, to me.

Wherever I wander, my love for thee traces
    Thy form in the shadows and leaves of each tree,
While fancy reflects from all beautiful faces
    Susannah, Susannah, Susannah, to me.

SUSANNAH.

Thou art my master of musical measures,
    Creator of worlds where my thought loves to roam ;
I'll be thy slave and preserve all thy treasures
    Of passion, and fashion my heart for their home.

ELNATHAN.

The world is aglow with the gladness of living:
  No hour of the past or of ages to be
Can match with this moment which sparkles in giving
  Susannah, Susannah, Susannah, to me.

KALBA, *entering*.

I met two men who had been sent
  By Joseph's son to make request
That, as the day is nearly spent,
  We should afford them food and rest.

ABSALOM.

Of course, your well-known liberality
Would offer ready hospitality:
At least no weary one, in want and need,
Would lack your pious blessing and God-speed.

KALBA.

I never give to beggars, or bestow
My alms on strangers whom I do not know.
I might, perchance, receive a rogue or rake.

ABSALOM.

Or entertain an angel by mistake.

KALBA.

But listen: those of whom I tell
Were going to the Harvest Feast,
When all the demon powers which dwell
In Jews appear to be released,
And building booths of myrtle boughs
Defile the night with wild carouse,
With dance and song and maddening din,
And, Jew-like, revel in their sin.

ABSALOM.

I saw no sin defile the night or day;
But holy mirth and innocence held sway.

KALBA.

Thou fool, when Shechem triumphs, thou wilt lose
Thy share through sinful sympathy with Jews.

JESUS, *entering with his followers.*

Oh, see how the night is approaching ;
Already the shades are encroaching
   Upon the dominion of day :
The night-wind is rising and blowing ;
The night-chill is stealthily sowing
   The seeds of decline and decay.

Attend to the voice of our pleading
In merciful kindness ; and, heeding
   The prayer of the poor and distrest,
But grant us in pity at least
A morsel of food from your feast
   And shelter wherein we may rest.

JOHN.

See, my master, they remain
   In sullen silence, nor reply ;
Therefore let our prayers constrain
   A fiery vengeance from on high,
As Elijah caused it rain
   Upon his foes in days gone by.

JESUS.

Not thus, but with a mind of peace,
   Shall we remove their mute disdain ;
And, manlike, loving man, release
   The heart of man from hate and pain.

ZADOK.

Then why do you, spurning this mountain of God,
   Propose to attend at that Temple of Shame,
Detested and noted, at home and abroad,
   For evil reports which still cling to its name ?

JESUS.

I go as herald of an age new born
   Whose sons and daughters wake from woe to be
Delivered from the night of grief and scorn
   Which clouded helpless guilt and poverty.

I go to make a pathway, paved with hearts
　　That bleed, to reach a throne of peace and light,
Before whose love and power all ill departs
　　And seeks to shroud itself in endless night.

ABSALOM.

Dost thou think to establish a kingdom of God, and ascend
　　To a throne and a crown in the peace and the joy of the world?
What could'st thou, a poor peasant, unaided, accomplish to lend
　　A glory to clouds which the armies of death have unfurled?
Canst thou say to the weak in the wasting of body and mind,
　　Be thou healed of the plague and endowed with a vigorous soul?
Canst proclaim to the slaves as they languish, repressed and confined,
　　You are loosed from your fetters and freed from the tyrant's control?
Wilt thou gather the children together within such a fold
　　That the demons in men be unable to fashion the chain
Which they forge of the whispers of sin and destroy, taking hold
　　Of the fancy of youth and corrupting its heart and its brain?
And the man who is paying the price of inherited sin,
　　And the woman abandoned and lost for the love of an hour,
And the naked, and hungry, and dying, and dead, canst thou win
　　To renewal of life by the sway of this coveted power?

JESUS.

Yes; for love is almighty and able to fling
Round the winter of life the renewal of spring,
And in shedding its riches around on the poor
Is creating a power that shall ever endure.

NABAL.

But why preserve the weak who still oppose
The progress of the race, its constant foes?
'Tis better each should seek his own delight,
Enjoy the day ere passing into night.

JESUS.

If love should lose the life of love, and seek
　　Its own and not another's happiness,
　　It would, self-sacrificing, gain no less
And win the riches which await the meek.

F

Nor shall the great rewards of Heaven speak
   Alone, declaring love's assured success ;
   For, in the coming age, the race shall bless
The hand that helped when it was worn and weak.

But what reward could weigh with this, to know
   That heart responds to heart ; that kindly tongue
Can wake love's gentle echoes, till a glow
   Of faith inspires the spirit, wrought and wrung :
That simple words of love can lighten woe
   As much as sweetest song by psalmist sung ?

ABSALOM.

We have poisoned the dayspring of love with a diet
   Composed of our hatred and lust,
Till our lives have no light but the rancour and riot
   Consuming our manhood to dust.

We demand, and we pray, and implore some distraction
   From devils beneath and above ;
And we're fain to relieve the long tension of action
   With lies of religion or love.

And the terrors of day and of nightfall are equal ;
   The cup is o'erflowing with gall,
Which we take at the hands of the darkness as sequel
   Of all that is done by us all.

The delights which were sweet to our childhood are acid ;
   And wearied of virtue and vice,
We can look on the horrors of hell-fire as placid
   And pleasure that's cheap at the price.

ELNATHAN, *to Jesus.*

Be sovran in the world of song
Because thy tone, sincere and strong,
Can sway the feelings of the heart
With power beyond my humble art ;
And take my wreath, the poet's crown ;
Before thy feet I lay it down.

SUSANNAH.

Yes, Jesus, reign and satisfy the longing,
   Born of toil that lives and hope that dies away :
Reign, while, around thee, youths and maidens thronging
   Hail the dawning of the new and brighter day.

See, we would pierce the fateful curtain hiding
    What the future holds, but rashly turn aside
To dream of golden ages past, confiding
    In the monuments that minister to pride.

Be prophet of the future, realising
    All of him, of whom the prophet Moses told,
Who comes restoring all things and surprising
    Men with peaceful sway and splendours manifold.

NABAL.

Aye, so the trees besought the bramble's aid,
    As Jotham said so many years ago,
To form a kingdom, and beneath its shade
    They'd screen themselves from all the winds that blow.

JUDAS.

Not here, not here, but where those world-famed splendours
    Once crowned the throne of Judah's mighty king,
Thy name shall be enrolled with our defenders
    Whom village-maids and temple-psalmists sing.

MARY.

O Jesus, hearken to my prayer,
    And come away in haste with me :
Dost thou not see how they prepare
    A trap and snare to ruin thee ?

By every pang a mother bears,
    By all the anguish she must know,
Oh, listen to my earnest prayers
    And come, and we shall homeward go.

I'll tend thee as in days of yore,
    And thou once more shalt sit by me
With smiles, like those thy features wore
    In days before this enmity.

Oh, thou canst not refuse me still,
    Nor harshly view thy mother's tears,
But choose the path which may fulfil
    The hopes that grew with all thy years.

JESUS.

Where the prophets told their vision,
Meeting scorn and foul derision,
There I must fulfil my mission,
    Though a fate like theirs be mine.

Still about me darkness, throwing
Shadows on my path, is growing;
Yet, beyond, the world is glowing
    Where the suns of freedom shine.

ZADOK.

Then leave us, feeble, false and faithless one;
And when thy short and shameless course is run,
Recall the day we offered thee the light,
When thou didst choose the path of sin and night.
Thy name shall lead the ever-lengthening roll
Of men, depraved in mind and lost in soul,
Who pass this holy shrine nor heed the claims
Of wondrous works and patriarchal names.
Then go, and find with sinners such a doom
As tortures thee alive and haunts thy tomb.

ELNATHAN.

Thou star of the morning, though veiled in the mist and o'ercloud
Like life in its budding which sorrows and terrors have shrouded,
Art herald of Man; and the dawn of his kingdom is breaking,
For God in the truth and the hope of mankind is awaking.

JESUS.

Sing, poet, sing, to thee the voice is given;
    Celebrate the day of God, which gleams from far,
When darkness dies away and clouds are riven
    By the splendour filling all without a bar.

Sing, poet, sing the thoughts and dreams of ages,
    Till those dreams become a hope, and hope a fact:
Sing with a soaring soul and find thy wages
    In the faith that heroes heed thy voice and act.

ABSALOM, to Jesus.

Thou would'st make of his measures the pivots
    Of action and thought,
And create of his fancies the rivets
    For frames that are wrought
To support a false faith but outlive its
    Pursual of naught.

As for me, I would hurl a defiance
    At faiths which are strong,
And refuse to endure a compliance
    With dreams which prolong
The subjection of reason and science
    To story and song.

Yet the reason of man is benighted
    And sees not the light,
But is watching the world-ways, affrighted,
    And cowers at the sight,
Though its pride has encountered and slighted
    The Truth and the Right.

NABAL, to Jesus.

Begone, and let thine evil dream enthrall
    Thy soul, and may its tendrils round thee twine,
And bear thee golden fruit but sour as gall,
    Like that which hangs upon the Dead Sea vine.

JOHN.

Thy path of pain and death in cold disdain
Shall win the world to worship and attain
    A calmer splendour than the starry spaces,
    While Art shall yield her life of loves and graces
To mark with triumph-song and princely fane
    Thy path of pain.

Then greed shall kindle minds of men insane
With hope to grasp the crown of God and gain
    A throne like thine where selfishness embraces
    Thy path of pain.

But thou shalt live and watch the endless train
Of lives whose love of light shall prove their bane,
  And in the passion pictured in their faces
  Thy soul of truth and sacrifice retraces
With broken heart that bleeds in vain, in vain,
  Thy path of pain.

ABSALOM.

Are sorrow and anguish supreme and eternal,
  That thou would'st contrive of them scaffolds to raise
A shrine which surpasses the virile and vernal
  Live temples the sun-god creates for his praise
  Of all of the gladness his glory surveys ?

Proclaim with the clamour of failing conviction
  The beauty of palsy and bounty of pain,
Till the world is bewitched with the charm of the fiction,
  And spurns its delight with religious disdain
  To worship its sorrow with darkness for fane.

SCENE 6.—The Court of the Women, in the Temple.

(A marble wall is built upon the west,
  In which is set Nicanor's splendid gate
  With doors of massive bronze ; and wondrous weight
Of gold and silver ornaments the rest.

Men climb by fifteen steps, and on their breast
  They bow the head, and stand in humble state,
  Before they lift their eyes to view the great
And holy altar, once by heroes blest.

Above the whitened altar nobly towers
  The House of God, of marble, pure and fine ;
The sun beyond ; its rays, with weakened powers,
  Upon the golden pinnacles still shine ;
And, in the porch, the grape of gold embowers
  A veil whose hues and figures intertwine.)

   BARUK, *a priest, to Alexander.*

A weird despair at times will hold possession
  Of heart and life, and desolate my soul ;
And thoughts, the sires and children of depression,
  League with the mind's impatience of control.

My faith is gone, the spirit wildly yearning
  To see my God enthroned above the world,
The passion loathing sensuous love and spurning
  All else than spheres where Truth's pure scroll's unfurled.

Those dreams are dead ; and winter-storms succeeding
    The placid strength of summer's smiling seas,
I view myself in victims, bound and bleeding,
    And curse the God whom savage rites appease.

I looked, but looked in vain, to find some token
    That men inherit immortality,
To know what laws eternal Right had spoken,
    And gain some proof of God's reality.

The teachers bade me bow my head and hearken
    To fables they had formed from ancient lies:
They sought to quench within my soul and darken
    The flame which gleamed in passion from mine eyes.

At last, of any certainty despairing,
    Beholding all my search to find it fail,
My heart, impelled by blind and reckless daring,
    Resolved to pass by stealth within the Veil.

But vain my hope, nor could my step unsaintly
    Arouse the guardian of the sacred shrine ;
No glory flamed in fire or flickered faintly,
    But darkness such as fills this soul of mine.

I prayed to God for any wild conviction,
    For any mission that a god could give ;
I cried with tears to spare me this affliction,
    Without an aim, without a hope, to live.

ALEXANDER.

Courage, sir, the future opens brightly ;
    See what splendours gather round the Jewish name ;
All this Temple's glory must delight thee,
    Built by Herod's favour, crowned with priestly fame.

Now the men of other climes and races
    Read the sacred scrolls and keep the ancient Law,
Come to pay their vows within these places,
    For of God's great name the heathen stand in awe.

BARUK.

Herod's favour, boast most glorious ;
    Let the sons of Jacob shout for joy ;
Thus does Esau reign victorious ;
    Why should ancient memories annoy ?

When, as captives, spoiled by strangers,
  Joseph's rebel children left this land,
By her tomb to view their dangers
  Rachel's mournful ghost was seen to stand.

Clouds again are onward creeping;
  Now again the heathen laws oppress;
Never ghost is heard in weeping;
  No one deigns to pity our distress.

ALEXANDER.

Yet there is reason for joy,
  Seeing the signs of these days;
We shall our voices employ,
  Hailing the Prophet with praise.

Then shall the sceptre return,
  Wielded by mightier hand;
Wrath, without mercy and stern,
  Fall on the foes of the land.

BARUK.

The age of wonders long has ceased;
  No more with awe inspired,
  No more with ardour fired,
Men see Immortals at their feast.

In ruder times it found belief
  That gods and ghosts appeared;
  And patient hearts were cheered,
Who thought they came for their relief.

But now, grown wise, we know too well
  Naught cares for our estate;
  For, puppets of dead fate,
We pass to nothingness through hell.

ALEXANDER.

Canst thou thus translate
All thy love and hate
Into lifeless fate?

Didst thou never know
Hate like hell below,
Love's impassioned glow?

BARUK.

Yes; I have known emotion, fierce and wild,
  Which whirled me with its torrent force,
A passionate devotion, undefiled
  By thought that flowed from selfish source.

A woman looked on me, and from her eyes
  Pure love flashed forth in radiant light,
And, as a song will wake the world's surprise,
  It broke in morning o'er my night.

But who could paint the eager longing,
  The secret rapture of the first wild kiss,
The tumult of the passions thronging
  To taste the sweetness of such matchless bliss?

The world grew young; in mystic fashion
  The voice of earth below and sky above
Was tremulous with tearful passion
  And sang in loudest strain the song of love.

JUDAS, *to Jesus, as they enter with others.*

  Master, how the spirit glows
    In gazing on such scenes as these,
  Where each rite and structure shews
    The power of ancient memories.

  There the tablets still record
    How Judas, named the Hammer, fought
  For the people of the Lord
    With strength and valour passing thought.

BARUK, *to Alexander.*

  How strangely sad that face,
  As if the soul within
  Was swayed by some dim dream
  And lighted by a gleam
  Of glories, such as grace
  A victor over sin.

ALEXANDER.

  I have often met him here,
    Followed by that peasant throng;
  They, as held with silent fear;
    He, as soul-possessed with song.

Like a psalm, at times his speech
    Strikes in music on the ear,
Rousing souls with tones that reach
    Through the darkness of their fear.

BARUK, *to Simon, a pharisee, who enters.*

Peace be with thee, stranger; who is he
Followed by the crowd from Galilee?

SIMON, *a pharisee.*

A man who left his occupation,
    Assured that he, untaught, could rule
Our lives with paltry speculation
    Uncountenanced by rabbi's school.

Those creatures of the soil will travel
    For miles to lend him lengthened ears;
And, as he talks, his tiresome cavil
    Subverts their faith with foolish tears.

JUDAS, *to Jesus.*

Now occasion waits for thee;
    A thousand zealots throng the place;
Strike for God and liberty,
    Or die a dastard in disgrace.

JESUS.

Shall I, a nobler crown desiring,
And to a greater throne aspiring,
Forsake the path that I have trod
In happy fellowship with God,
And reign o'er those whom passions lead
To violence in word and deed?

JUDAS.

Must thou still drug thy soul with dreams
    In face of all the times demand;
Or wilt thou frame a sober scheme
    To form a kingdom in this land?

JESUS.

Oh, how sweet are the joys of the bosom which knows
    And which glows
With the vast love of God ; all that love which bestows
    On the throes
Of the spirit such value that surely appears
    After years,
In its gladness, the soul which was purged by its fears
    And its tears.

And how sweet are the joys of the bosom which feels
    And reveals
How the deep love of man so much misery heals,
    And appeals
To the Father of all that he hasten the day
    When his sway
Shall extend o'er the world and all wrong pass away
    In decay.

JUDAS.

A man immured in life's cold prison
    Will beat upon the dead stone walls,
Till o'er his head a light has risen
    And through a narrow opening falls.

Then patiently he leans to hearken
    What message comes from worlds above,
And thinks no more of walls which darken
    His world of happiness and love.

While we admire his resignation,
    Commend his piety and grace,
Our teachers prove God's visitation
    Has lightened all the cruel place.

Break, break with me the walls confining
    Our race in gloom and poverty,
For sure the ray, now feebly shining,
    Will blaze upon the man when free.

JESUS.

By self-control and many pains
    The prophet-soul attains
The vantage-ground from which it sees
    The battle with disease,

The beauteous bloom of bounteous health,
   The witchery of wealth,
And all that war of love and hate
   Which works a mortal's fate.

One welcomed blast of selfish breath
   Can darken dreams with death,
And scorch with fire of foulest flame
   The soul that shrank from shame,
Bequeathing memory a stench
   With power to quell and quench
The furnace of such pure desire
   As robes e'en God in fire.

BARUK, to *Alexander*.

Her nervous grace reveals a soul in storm,
And lends an eloquence to speechless form.
Her lustrous eyes, in which her spirit shines,
Are veiled by lashes dark ; in pencilled lines
Her eye-brows meet ; and round her forehead, low
But smooth, and white as newly fallen snow,
She wears a golden band ; and from it droops
On both her brows the jewel-chain, in loops
Which link beneath her soft and rounded chin.
Red lips and pearly teeth seem framed within
The golden circlet pendent on her face.
Her raven tresses flow with richest grace
In rippling streams beneath the veil that, down,
A silken cloud, floats from her golden crown.
About her neck the pearl and coral chains
Depend in rows, and vainly each restrains
The heaving and the throbbing of her breast,
Scarce hidden by the white embroidered vest.
And then her hands, so gentle and so white,
So small and delicate, are bathed in light
Which flashes from her rings. Her sleeves made wide
Display her full-shaped arms, my darling's pride,
Adorned with bracelets ; but the chains suggest
The bonds of one imprisoned and distrest.
And both her ears their veil of jewels wear,
Like golden grapes in clusters, ripe and rare.
With great and costly shoulder-clasps confined,

Her purple mantle falls in folds behind.
Her linen girdle, wrought in fashion chaste,
Is wound in many folds about her waist,
And binds the crimson tunic, richly gemmed
With pearls and jewels and with border hemmed
In deepest purple; while the flowing train
Is trimmed with gold; and, as she moves, a strain
Most sweet of laughing, tinkling music tells
She shakes and wakes her silver ankle-bells.

ALEXANDER.

I have seen the high-priest's daughter,
  But her eyes were clear from care;
Bright with smiles, none would have thought her
  Maid in passionate despair.

BARUK.

There's a sorrow that sleeps in the smiling
  Of faces that feign
To be gladdened and gleesome, beguiling
  With patience their pain.

There's a sadness that sobs in the speeches
  Of spirits that smart,
And its rhythm and rhetoric reaches
  The heart of the heart.

ANNAS, SON OF ANNAS, *entering with others*.

As councillors, we make demand
  Who gave to thee a rab's commission;
Art thou the prophet of the land;
  Or one who dares to sow sedition?

JESUS.

When John baptised,
Who authorised
The course he ran:
Did God or man?

ANNAS, SON OF ANNAS, *to his companions*.

We cannot say that John the Baptist had
His power from God, for we supposed him mad.

ALEXANDER.

Nor can we say, Of men, lest they be stirred
To wrath, who heard and hearkened to his word.

ANNAS, SON OF ANNAS.

No one knows.

JESUS.

And neither will I seek
To disclose
Who bestows
On me the power to speak.

JESUS, *seating himself on the steps.*

Behold a lord, whom wealth and power incline
To hedge a field and plant a chosen vine ;
He builds a tower and vat to press the wine.

He hires some tillers, men who understand
The culture of the grape, and to their hand
Commits the field ; and seeks a distant land.

And, afterwards, he sends a slave to say
That they must give the fruits without delay :
They answer him with blows, nor will obey.

The lord is wroth, and sends another slave ;
And he, dishonoured, scarce his life can save :
A third they kill, nor grant him e'en a grave.

The lord affirms, No messengers remain,
Except my well-loved son ; but he'll obtain
Like reverence with myself, nor go in vain.

And, seeing him, the murderous tillers say,
It is the heir ; the field becomes our prey
When he is dead : they cast him forth and slay.

The lord returns, the sword of wrath to bear
Against the rebels: none of them he'll spare,
But give the vineyard into others' care.

For have ye never e'en this scripture read :
The stone refused becomes the corner's head ?
So God appoints, and we are filled with dread.

ANNAS, SON OF ANNAS.

Are we the murderous tillers, prophet-slaying,
  Whom God condemns because we have displeased him?

SIMON, *a pharisee*.

But leave him now, his punishment delaying;
  The pilgrims would be angered if we seized him.

ALEXANDER.

Then, of himself, he quotes the psalmist's saying
  Concerning Israël who serves in pain :
He also claims Messiah's throne, arraying
  Himself as Judah's son who comes to reign.

SIMON, *a pharisee*.

No puny throne suffices his ambition;
  To rule this land would rouse his deep disdain,
For God the Lord has given him a mission
  To drag all kings and Cæsars in his train.
Approach and question: he has no suspicion.

ALEXANDER.

We know that thou art true, and teachest true;
That fearless thou dost view our sad condition:
  Dost thou regard the tax as Cæsar's due?

JESUS.

Why do ye set a snare for me?
  But bring a coin that I may tell.
Now whose the face that here we see;
  And whose the name these letters spell?

ALEXANDER.

The name and face are Cæsar's, as they say,
  And his alone.

JESUS.

The due of Cæsar unto Cæsar pay,
  To God his own.

JESUS, *to John*.

Come, my lad, repeat the verses
  Which king David sang of old,
Words in which the king rehearses
  What the future times unfold.

JOHN.

Eternal God has clearly spoken
   Unto my lord who reigns as king :
Behold thy foes, their forces broken,
   Their tribute unto thee shall bring ;
And, round thy throne, the people, thronging,
   Are robed as on a festive day,
While youthful breasts are filled with longing
   To follow thee in war-array.

And thine shall be the priestly glory
   Of him who ruled within this place ;
For, like that king of ancient story,
   Thou art a priest of endless race.
Behold, at length, in rage awaking,
   The sceptred Lord of Sabaoth ;
And all the thrones, in terror shaking,
   Shall plight to thee their trembling troth.

JESUS.

How say ye, scribes, that God's Anointed
   From David's royal line shall spring,
The psalmist's child is he appointed
   To reign on David's throne as king ;
For, as he spoke, the lad was telling
   How David wrote of God's award
Which crowns a greater king, compelling
   The world to yield to David's lord ?

SIMON, *a pharisee.*

Dost thou mock us ? Then beware
Of the fate which we'll prepare
For thee, that thy name may be
Term of scorn and infamy ;
Till the sound is only heard
As a shameful, whispered word.
Vilest memories shall cling
Round thee as a loathsome thing,
As an idle, worthless knave,
Buried in a borrowed grave.

JESUS, *rising.*

Avoid such men as those ; the scribe, who wears
    A woman's robes which trail upon the ground,
And, strutting like some noble damsel, stares
    With conscious pride on humbler men around,
And grins when any passer-by prepares
    To meet his glance with reverence profound.

Beware the pharisee, who binds the law
    In parchment case upon his brow and hand,
Who found his joy when lowly mortals saw
    Him, at the corner of the market, stand
With hands uplifted, while his leathern jaw
    Proclaimed to God his pleasure and command.

With solemn face and robber-hands they seize
    The widow's house, her children's bread, and sell
Their ill-got prey ; and, like some fell disease,
    They live upon their victims' loss, and swell
With others' food : there wait for such as these
    A sterner judgment and a fiercer hell.

SCENE 7.—The House of Joseph, called Caiaphas, the High-Priest.

(THE guest-room lamps flame overhead
And throw their light on carpets, spread
To furnish forth a proud display,
And couches set in due array.
But, through the pillars which support
The cloister-roofs, appears the court
Illumined by the full-orbed moon;
And from the porch the slave-girl's croon
Swells on the world with wistful tones,
Like shattered waves on shaken stones.)

LEAH, singing.

The stillness of the starry night
  Will lull those fevered thoughts to slumber,
Which blazing noon bequeathes to blight
The stillness of the starry night;
And when they palsy us with fright,
  Or throng like spectres none may number,
The stillness of the starry night
  Will lull those fevered thoughts to slumber.

HANNAH, entering.

I cannot rest; there is some evil brewing,
  And ills, unknown, have filled me with alarm.
Is Baruk safe? I wonder what he's doing.
  It cannot be that he is come to harm.

Why, Leah, are the lamps still burning,
  And all the house ablaze with light?

LEAH.

Thy father, lady, is returning
  To hold a council here to-night.

BARUK, *entering.*

Hannah!

HANNAH.

Baruk!

BARUK.

Soul of my soul, now fare you well:
  My hopes are gone, and darkness grows around me;
Broken and shattered is the spell
  Which, until now, in loving fetters bound me.

HANNAH.

  'Tis not pride that slays the maiden
    Whom her lover has forsaken;
  She is not with sorrow laden,
    Nor with trembling anger shaken.

  But her love, again returning
    To her bosom, is increasing;
  And the growing flame is burning,
    Burning ever, never ceasing.

  For the flame, in fierceness growing,
    Leaves its home, a victim needing;
  If it fails, returns, still glowing;
    Henceforth on its own heart feeding.

LEAH.

Lady, beware lest thy father surprise thee.
  I'll go and watch for his step at the gate.

HANNAH.

Go then, my Leah. And must I despise thee,
  Changing my love into bitterest hate?

BARUK.

  No; but my path has grown so dark,
    My strength and courage waver;
  For every human dog may bark
    At him who's out of favour.

I dare not shrine thy life in mine
    For which my fate is calling;
Nor should the vine delight to twine
    Around the oak in falling.

HANNAH.

If I could find thee the words which betoken
    Affection impassioned and panting in pain,
Then would my heart, in the hour it is broken,
    Compose thee its love-song and die in the strain.

Why I must love thee I make no inquiry,
    For mine is the reasonless love of a maid,
Love which is kindled in passion so fiery
    That heaven and happiness wither and fade.

Should'st thou deceive me, prove faithless and cruel,
    And be but an idol that curses its shrine,
Then I will make my affection the fuel
    And offer my life on the altar of thine.

BARUK.

Farewell, the chill of baffled hope is stealing
    Over my heart, and palsies hand and brain;
And that wild dream, which shone as if revealing
    The countless joys that crowd in Passion's train,
Now mocks my soul, no longer e'en concealing
    How hopeless all it called me to attain;
While, lost in dull amazement, Thought and Feeling
    Decline, decay and pass away in pain.

HANNAH.

Not youth cut off by sudden death,
    Or life in last retreat,
Can match a love-lorn maiden's breath
    In pathos of defeat.

BARUK.

The halo of youth, which delighted
    And circled the brow of the day,
Has passed from my life, which is blighted,
    For ever away.

Another, more happy, shall guide you
  To visions of virtue and truth,
And sing, as he marches beside you,
  The war-song of youth.

HANNAH.

The wave of the ocean, in dying
  In song on the stones of the beach,
Has never a music out-vying
  The tones of your speech.

BARUK.

The wind-wakened wave of the rivers,
  Which shivers in stress and surprise,
Is liker my spirit, which quivers,
  Delivers a murmur and dies.

HANNAH.

But I love thee. Dost thou doubt me?
  Never question love like mine:
Light of heaven flames about me
  When my hand is clasped in thine.

I'll forget my maiden blushes,
  And confess my love to thee,
Though some ancient maxim hushes
  Words which flow too fast and free.

Should my heart, in silence breaking,
  Hide its love nor dare to speak
Till, bereaved and lonely, waking
  To a life, forlorn and bleak?

BARUK.

Will of the world, who makest man's endeavour
  Seem but the strife of shadows with the sun,
Why must we toil from birth to death, but never
  Reign o'er the realm our work of war has won?

All of our life is spent and lost in gaining
  Truths that the distance decks with morning rays:
Lo, as we grasp them, they're already waning,
  Pallid as clouds on skies of chrysoprase.

Look on the waters when the light is flinging
    Flowerets of flame and leaves of ruddy gold ;
Wondrous the world of beauty there outspringing ;
    Touch it and see ! The stream is dark and cold.

Sunset is throned on pearl and lilac splendours
    Set in the stillness of an azure flood ;
Yet, as we look, the faithless glow surrenders
    Exquisite beauties in a blaze of blood.

HANNAH.

On every breeze a whispered word is flying,
    On every stream is written by the sun ;
Its name is woven in the splendours dyeing
    The tapestries of cloud and azure spun.

It cries athwart the crashing of the thunder,
    Descending with the lightning's flaming bolt ;
Screams in the rage that rends the skies asunder
    Till Earth and Heaven fever in revolt.

In noontide's heat it lies in letters brazen
    Upon the fiery sun's imperial plumes,
But flies to tread this lowly world and blazon
    The rhododendron's pallid purple blooms.

In every heart its murmurs are repeated,
    In waking eyes it trembles as a mist,
Purging the life of passions which defeated
    Sorrow, divine and vaunted exorcist.

It robes with flame the restless dreamer living
    To spurn submission and to strive with wrong,
And makes a mortal more than mortal, giving
    The love in music with the light in song.

Its sultry beams glare on the stern ascetic,
    And yet its radiance soothes the lover's soul,
Arraying each, as stars are energetic
    To wreathe the night with fading aureole.

Thou didst unfold it, mighty Maccabean,
    Crowned for the boon with battle's hurricane ;
But petty factions shout thy chant as pæan,
    And in their strife the word is lost again.

As men regard the runes of vanished races,
  We glance upon the hieroglyph unawed.
One moment! Now my spirit's free and traces
  The hidden meaning. Can the word be " God " ?

LEAH, *singing*.

But noon, transfigured in a dream
  Born of the haze in moonlit glances,
Bewitches men till passions seem
But noon transfigured in a dream ;
And mystified by fancy's gleam,
  They trace no truth in nightly trances,
But noon, transfigured in a dream
  Born of the haze in moonlit glances.

BARUK.

This gasp, this stare, what do they mean ?
  Then look upon these hands, and see ;
Grasping the void which lies between
  The prize that drew my life and me.

I fall, as one who sees the goal
  Scarcely elude his fingers' touch :
I faint, for that which thralled my soul
  Has only just escaped my clutch.

The fancies which transformed the earth
  And lit my dreams with lustrous light
Perished, as suddenly as dearth
  Of hope created hell and night.

Is there no other back to bear
  The blame that crowns my ill-success ;
No means to soothe my own despair
  By taunting God with faithlessness ?

And have I struggled all my days,
  Stumbled and fallen, risen, fought
So many times and scorned dispraise,
  To fail at last, attaining naught ?

Could I but stand before God's throne
    To speak my heart out to his face
And say to him, " Must I alone
    " Desire the good and gain disgrace ?

" Others have won both wealth and fame ;
    " Others have lived in laughing ease ;
" Mine is the broken-hearted shame
    " That Nature's smiles can ne'er appease.

" My fever grows : I would be calm
    " And reason with thee, but my heart
" Chants as an undersong this psalm,
    " Turgid and destitute of art :

" In darkness thou art ever near,
    " Although my senses can't perceive
" Thy ways or works, and doubting fear
    " Flies from the love to which I cleave.

" The clouds have veiled the vault of stars,
    " And coldness brings a frozen rest,
" But still thy hands with burning scars
    " Are laid upon my brow and breast.

" Thou dost not need my praise or prayer ;
    " I do not need thy praise or prize ;
" All that we need is everywhere,
    " The living love that satisfies."

The sun shall smile upon the grass,
    And play upon the pleasant streams
With joy whose radiancies surpass
    The visioned splendours of my dreams.

The seed shall fall upon the soil,
    And, in the shattering of its shell,
Waken to win by happy toil
    A fairer form than asphodel.

My heart was broken : now I know
    The motive which inspired the deed,
For only thus my life could grow
    To manhood from the prisoned seed.

HANNAH.

Despair had found thee lonely
    And fixed her livid stare,
Till every thought was only
    Despair.

For life seemed sad and lengthy,
    With whispers growing rife
That death's the sole nepenthe
    For life.

But light dissolves the subtle
    And steel-grey web that night
Enweaves with every shuttle
    But light.

As youth is ever surgent
    And fired with new-born truth,
So truth is yours and urgent
    As youth.

With hope a heart envigoured
    Finds in defeat but scope
For energies transfigured
    With hope.

For love, the laughing tyrant
    In dreams of worlds above,
Suspires in each aspirant
    For love.

And fame, now false and sterile,
    Shall welcome with acclaim
The man who mocked at peril
    And fame.

BARUK.

Through life's burnt soil my troubled fancy traces
    The footmarks left by lovers long ago ;
    And in the tracks my spirit learns to know
What storms and sun-bursts passioned in these places.

For see where time already half effaces
    Divergent paths and footfalls, sad and slow ;
    But yonder marks retain the morning glow
Of mingled spirits lightening desert spaces.

If through the mist suspended o'er these wastes,
    Imagination should divine fruition
Of dreams in which my lonely pathway hastes

To merge in yours, would you in anger ban
    The hopeful heart which found its full ambition
In weakly woman linked to frailer man?

HANNAH.

As a man in the praise of his brother,
    A poet in passionate song,
And a babe in the smile of its mother
    Is joyous and strong;

So the glance of a maid on her lover
    Endows with renewal of life,
And his spirit awakes to recover
    Its strength for its strife;

For the love which is strong to transfigure
    The form and the features of death
Can inspire with a holier vigour
    And fierier breath.

BARUK.

The night, which streams o'er yonder skies,
    Brings no alarm,
If light, which dreams upon your eyes,
    Bestow its charm
On heart in shrouds of woe and scorn
    And folds of earth,
Disparting clouds to shew the morn
    In golden birth.

HANNAH.

When you declared you loved me more than life,
    And I believed the tale so sweetly told,
I dreamed of days when I, a happy wife,
    Might tell my love through lips grown fondly bold.

But now my bosom will not be controlled,
Though it was hushed to peace nor thought of strife
When you declared you loved me more than life,
    And I believed the tale so sweetly told.

For thus you come again and bring a knife
   To cleave the hope which wraps me in its fold,
Until that future seem with sorrows rife,
   Which shone in light and blazed with gleaming gold
When you declared you loved me more than life,
   And I believed the tale so sweetly told.

BARUK.

The dawn in its beauty, englassing
   Its grace in the face of the sea,
Has never a beauty surpassing
   Your smiling for me.

The breeze, in its breathing the brightest
   Of songs on its harp of a tree,
Has never a tone like your lightest
   Of whispers for me.

And life, though it glow with tradition
   And sparkle with splendours to be,
Can never possess such a vision
   Of glory for me.

HANNAH.

The sun-beams and moon-gleams may dwindle
   And star-glitter tremble and flee,
But still will the fire which you kindle
   Be heaven for me.

BARUK.

My despair seems as yet undiminished;
   Its shadow will darken your days,
And will render our life-work unfinished,
   Unworthy of praise.

All the laughter of life will be lacking
   In strength for dispelling the smart,
When the dread of defeat will be racking
   My head and your heart.

HANNAH.

When Hope has grown dark as the beryl,
   And Fancy has paled to the lips,
When Reason is barren and sterile
   And veiled in eclipse,

Thy strength shall prove stronger than iron
   To strive and to wrestle with wrong,
For mine is the power to environ
   Thy soul with a song.

BARUK.

In the depth of the silence and darkness afar
There's unchangeable grouping of star upon star;
And though meteors flash and the night-winds be shrill,
Though the surges of ocean in night-tempest thrill,
Yet the fears they awaken are lulled into rest
By the peace of the stars on the firmament's breast;
So the darkness of life has no terrors for me
While the star-group of hope and affection shall be.

HANNAH.

There's a splendour which shines in the shimmer
   Of stars on a stream,
Which assumes to the sight of a swimmer
   The dimness of dream,
Like the glory of God; and the glimmer
   Of gold in the gleam
Still entrances his glances, while dimmer
   The shore-meadows seem.

So the faintest of flamelets is flashing
   On foam of the tide
Where the billows of being are dashing
   The swimmers aside,
While we look at the light which no splashing
   Or darkness can hide;
And we'll strive, spite of weeping and gnashing
   Of teeth, in our pride.

LEAH.

Thy father, lady, comes this way.
Oh, sir, begone without delay.

HANNAH.

I'll send thee word, if thou wilt wait
At dawn outside the Northern gate.

BARUK.
Farewell; my world bewails its loss of light.

HANNAH.
Farewell; my heart must hunger through the night.

LEAH.
Oh, what will happen should he find you here?
My lady, fly: I tremble, filled with fear.
(They go out in opposite directions.)

LEAH, <i>singing</i>.
The night has children of its own
   In ruthless hate and reckless passion;
And though the noon may hush its groan,
The night has children of its own
   To wreck its solemn monotone;
For, freed from frenzy noon-tides fashion,
The night has children of its own
   In ruthless hate and reckless passion.

JOSEPH, THE HIGH-PRIEST, <i>entering with Alexander</i>.
What man was he now passing out?

LEAH.
A priest who sought your lordship here.

THE HIGH-PRIEST.
The matter he had come about?

LEAH.
It was intended for your ear.

THE HIGH-PRIEST.
Yes; Alexander, one of those
Whom you, in your discretion, chose
To aid us execute our plan.

ALEXANDER.
Good sir, I saw the way he ran;
And it was Baruk I would swear.

THE HIGH-PRIEST.

What? Always Baruk. May I share
What waits for him, if I shall still
Refrain while he withstands my will!

ALEXANDER.

Your lady's father.

ANNAS, *entering with Joseph*.

Strike the blow
Whose force shall cause all men to know
That we, the rulers, take no share
In plots which zeal and fraud prepare.

THE HIGH-PRIEST.

I fear we choose an evil day;
For while the crowds of pilgrims stay
To hold the Feast, a small event
May rouse their sleeping discontent.

ALEXANDER.

When priests and statesmen bless a cause,
The people hail it with applause;
So bend this Pilate to our side,
And patriots then must run and hide.

THE HIGH-PRIEST.

And yet no patriot does he seem to be;
  He cursed the pharisees and all their school.

ANNAS.

Like them he dreams of Jewish realms set free
  From foreign tyrannies and Roman rule.

ALEXANDER.

He was no pharisee; nor yet, like you,
  Would serve the time that we might still be sure
Of Rome's caress; nor would he e'er pursue
  The plans of Herod. He is of the Poor.

THE HIGH-PRIEST.

And what could Herod's policy succeed
  In gaining for the state except the end
Of ancient laws? While Grecian rules would breed
  A host of ills.

ALEXANDER.

And you, you still pretend
To seek our good, to lull the crowd, nor wake
The Romans' wrath. Do you not undertake
A task beyond your power?

ANNAS.

These are not times
For factions in our midst, for now we call
The friends of law to rise and crush the crimes
And leaders of the Poor who threaten all.

JOSEPH.

Is it nothing to you that the people must strive
With the forces of nature that you may survive?
For the toilers are living the lives of the brutes
And perish, while you are enjoying the fruits.

Is it nothing to you that the labourer dies
And the children are swarming like swine in their sties,
While your mansions are built by the toil and the tears
Of the poor you repay with your smiles and your sneers?

ANNAS.

What words are those? Art thou too of the Poor?

ALEXANDER.

Poor wretch. He's crazed and mad, 'tis very sure.

ANNAS.

Our friends assemble.

THE HIGH-PRIEST.

They are welcome here.

ANNAS, SON OF ANNAS, *entering*.

Look, Jesus and the crowd are drawing near.

JOSEPH.

But, sirs, let us be careful what we do,
Lest we should, in our calmer moments, rue
A hasty act. There is no doubt the land
Is much disturbed; but then this helpless band

Of peasants is a very feeble sign
Of stronger, deeper plots which undermine
The social fabric ; so 'tis scarcely wise
   To crush the weak and nurse the secret foe.

ANNAS, SON OF ANNAS.

This Jesus trades in fables and in lies :
   His piety is but a market-show.

JOSEPH.

Nay ; keep those terms to style thy friends.   I heard
This Galilean speak such words as stirred
Those depths within the heart, which never feel
The unavailing rage of party-zeal ;
And from his lips would flow, with heat intense,
The lava-streams of fiery eloquence,
Which buried fear and falsehood in a tomb,
But furnished soil where truth and hope may bloom.

ANNAS.

That very power of speech makes him the more
The mouth-piece of the rebels who deplore
Our fallen state.

JOSEPH.

   Good sir, there is some cause
Since we must feel the curse of heathen laws.

ANNAS.

No doubt, the heathen strangers' reign
   Insults our God and Holy Place ;
But what can restless schemers gain
   Except the ruin of the race ?

ANNAS, SON OF ANNAS.

The Romans, roused to wrath, descry
   The hopes by which this sect is buoyed.

THE HIGH-PRIEST.

Then better this one man should die
   Than all the nation be destroyed.

ALL, *as Jesus enters with the Crowd.*

>He comes, the blasphemer,
>The heathen, the dreamer,
>The scorner of sages,
>Rejecting what ages
>Hand down by tradition.
>He boasts a commission
>From God, and with lying
>Insults the Undying.

JOSEPH.

Hear me a moment. Consider the work ye engage in, the
    aim ye pursue ;
Lest, in a time that is coming, your sons and your
    daughters, afflicted, shall rue
Woes which shall spring from this night; and perchance,
    for who knows all the future ? they'll see
In the defeat of this Jesus, the fall of the people he taught
    to be free.

Still at the gates of the future the spirit of mortals is
    busily beating,
Beats while it waits for the flinging apart of the portals
    and vision of peace,
Filling, meanwhile, and renewing its heart with its hope,
    and preparing a greeting,
Greeting of mortals immortal who long for a kingdom that
    never shall cease.

While they are waiting, and craving, and seeking a
    freedom from evil and sorrow,
Blighting the brain and the heart of them, clings the
    inherited sin of the ages,
Smiling its hate, and enslaving the weakness which flees
    from its reason to borrow
Light that has waned and departed, and brings from their
    merited rest the dead sages.

Still are the Past and the Present, with sins which were
    born at the birth or created
By the delusions and errors of living, defiling the purest
    endeavour,

Chilling and blasting the pleasant and winsome adornments
    of earth-dreams which waited
End of confusions and terrors while giving a smile that
    endureth for ever.
Shall we not honour the man who would call us to see in
    the Future a splendour
Such as the Past and the Present, though filled with their
    wealth, are unable to render?
Shall we not honour the man who can paint with a glory
    the darkness which shrouds
All of our lives, their beginning and end, in a vesture of
    sorrowful clouds?

ALEXANDER.

The beams of hope will tinge with golden glow
And paint with sunny hues the clouds which throw
Their shadows on our minds, until they wear
A drapery of splendid, witching grace;
But yet those clouds enveil the azure space
Which lies far off, in peace serenely fair.
Then let this dreamer die as one who fed
The people with false hopes, and in the stead
Of truth, the stern and sober face of truth,
Would have us love the dreams of idle youth.

ANNAS, SON OF ANNAS.

I do not understand these men. 'Tis time
To crush this sinner and erase his crime.

ANNAS.

Come, seat yourselves, my friends; we'll soon dispose
Of this, our work. Now let the man, who knows
This fellow's doings, come and in due course
Relate the same.

ANNAS, SON OF ANNAS.

        He said that he would force
The Jews to pay a tribute to our foes,
The Romans. Further, he declared that we
Should pay the tax.

ALEXANDER.

Not so; he said he'd free
The Jews from Rome; and I have heard him say
That he would claim the Jewish throne and slay
The men who would not own him as their lord.

LEAH, *in the courtyard, to Simon.*

Didst thou not follow Jesus? Oh, thou hast forgot
Thou wast of those who trusted him.

SIMON, *the Rock.*

No; I was not.

THE HIGH-PRIEST.

Then answer thou, of God and man abhorred,
What didst thou teach? And who were those who sought
Thy words?

JESUS.

I spoke to all the world, and taught
In synagogue and Temple, where the Jews
Assemble always. I have never wrought
In secret. These can tell, if they will choose,
What words I spoke, and what the hope I brought.

ALEXANDER, *striking him.*

Dost thou so answer God's High-priest?

JESUS.

If I spoke evil in the least,
Then testify. If well, then know
It was not thine to smite me.

ALEXANDER.

Oh!
Come, who were those who followed thee?
Thou villain, why dost thou delay?

LEAH, *in the courtyard, to Simon.*

Thou wast with him of Galilee.

SIMON, *the Rock.*

I understand not what you say.

ALEXANDER.

I heard him boast that he should reign
  O'er realms whose glories never wane,
And, with a power none e'er possessed,
  He'd give the earth an age of rest.

ANNAS, SON OF ANNAS.

'Tis true. 'Tis true ; and I have heard him say
  He'll pull the Temple down to build again.

ALEXANDER.

Not so, my friend. He said that he would lay
  The Temple in the dust and raise a fane
Without the aid of hands, for he possessed
  The power of God to make or to consume.

THE HIGH-PRIEST.

Dost answer nothing ? What do these attest ?

ALEXANDER.

No word. He sees the justice of his doom.

THE HIGH-PRIEST.

Hear ; I adjure thee by the living God
  That thou declare to us if thou art he
Whom God, whose majesty we praise and laud,
  Anointed king of worlds that are to be.

JESUS.

I am ; and ye shall see the Son of Man
  Enthroned in power and coming in the skies
To reign and quench the flame which passions fan,
  To kindle fire of love which never dies.

THE HIGH-PRIEST, *standing and rending his robes*.

What need we further witness ? Ye have heard
His utterance and God-reviling word.
What think ye ?

ALL, *standing and rending their robes*.

He is guilty. Let him die.

ALEXANDER, *flinging his coat over Jesus' head.*
Who smote thee, God's anointed? Prophesy.

LEAH, *in the courtyard, pointing to Simon.*
He was a member of the band.

SIMON, *the Rock.*
I understand not what you say.

BOAZ, *a labourer.*
Yes. Yes; 'tis true. I saw thee stand
  With others by him in the fray.

SIMON, *the Rock.*
I do not know the man of whom ye speak.

BOAZ.
Thou art a Galilean; as thy speech
Would prove.

SIMON, *the Rock.*
  May God do so to me, and wreak
  Like woes on me, if I have heard him teach,
Or followed him, or know the man at all.

ALEXANDER, *to the Priests.*
Now, let's away to Pilate's judgment-hall.

ANNAS.
'Tis cock-crow now. We needs must wait till day
Shall break; so bid our officers to stay
Till dawn; then we'll arraign him at the seat
Of judgment, and our work shall be complete.

JUDAS, *entering.*
The man is guiltless; take your dross accursed,
  And with it take my curses, strong and deep:
My soul, in floods of wild remorse immersed,
  Perceives eternal darkness o'er me creep.
If God could hear, I'd weary him with cries
To blast you with the vengeance of the skies.

ANNAS.

We do not care.
'Tis thine affair.

JUDAS.

Ah, God; the curse from Heaven falls and blights
   My life, my soul, my hope in God's Anointed;
And wrath, far worse than Hell, appals and lights
   With lurid flames the woes for me appointed.

The Vale of Hinnom, where the worm and fire
   For ever live and taint the gloomy air,
Is Paradise to what my dreams conspire
   To paint the world, a mirror of despair.

ALEXANDER.

While the world, in careless gladness,
Smiled upon his daring madness,
   Thou didst follow Jesus in the way.
Now the world, no longer smiling,
Round him rages, throngs, reviling,
   Thou for wages dost the man betray.

JUDAS.

The days of my youth were absorbed in a vision :
   I dreamed that I saw, through the veiling of time,
The isles to the Lord render willing submission,
   And Judah's proud sceptre in splendour sublime.

And Jesus, I thought, would have led us to glory,
   Accustomed to sway simple hearts by a word,
And able to win by a commonplace story
   The love of the crowd who adored as they heard.

I saw with delight he possessed an attraction
   For those whose wild spirits all dangers would brave;
Till, wroth with his schemes and his dreaming inaction,
   I sold him to you for the price of a slave.

And now, from my life has departed for ever
   The dream of my youth which had led me astray,
And with it the flame and the fire of endeavour
   For ever, for ever, have vanished away.

I fear not the torture wherein I am fated
    For ever, for ever, for ever, to dwell :
Already my soul in itself has created
    The hell of remorse, the most horrible hell.

I go from the world which disowns me, bequeathing
    The tale of a crime and the wreck of a name :
Already I see how its hatred is wreathing
    My brow with a halo of infamous shame.

I go ; for my heart is benumbed with its terror ;
    My soul is consumed with the horrible dread
Of meeting him, slain by my crime and your error,
    Whenever I pass to the world of the dead.

SCENE 8.—Before the Tower of Anthony.

(AGAINST the northern sky stands forth the tower
 With massive battlements and strong grey walls ;
 In front, the stone-built platform bids the thralls
Of Rome to think upon their judge, and cower.

Upon the right, the pale and growing power
 Of Dawn is opening wide the glorious halls
 Of Day, whose light in lavish splendour falls
On life renewed in trembling heart and flower.

The steps of ruddy Dawn in slowness creep
 Across the pearly haze, while Morning strews
Its path with radiance, spread as crimson deep
 And rosy gold with pale and azure blues
To where the West, which lies in sluggard sleep,
 Reflects with pallid smiles those varied hues.)

TITUS, *a soldier, to Cornelius.*

There is some Jewish plot in hand
This night, for I have seen a band
With torches cross the town. I know
That, at this feast, their passions grow
Beyond control of tongue or hand.

CORNELIUS, *a centurion.*
Excited feelings mark this land.

TITUS.
And yet the crowds in Rome can rage as they.

CORNELIUS.

'Tis true; yet Roman wrath will pass away
Before some timely gift; but these men die
To save their god from wrong.

TITUS.

          They cheat and lie
Enough to save the gods of all the world;
But it were well if Jews and gods were hurled
To hell for then these civil broils would cease.

CORNELIUS.

Not ease and pleasant peace
  Can nurse the human heart,
Or give to men release
  From sorrow and its smart.
The heroes of the earth
  Are those who waken strife
In which we see the birth
  Of higher, nobler life.
But he who strives to break
  The chains which curb our minds
Will see his work awake
  The wrath of slaves and hinds.
And cowards stand to gaze,
  Who in their heart admire
The cruelty which slays
  The hero's heart of fire.
Perhaps the Jewish soul
  Which scorns its slavery
Shall lead us to the goal
  Of noblest bravery.

TITUS.

Your heroes, by your gods, are coming here:
The noise grows louder.

CORNELIUS.

          Let the guard appear.
The sight of them will check the crowd, should they
Attempt a riot. Make a great display.

THE CROWD, *entering with Jesus.*

Away with him ! The cross ! The cross, I say !
Let him be crucified ! Away ! Away !

CORNELIUS.

Keep silence there. What do ye seek
In coming here ? Now you, sir, speak.

THE CROWD.

Away with him, the rogue ; and let him die !
Away, and crucify him ! Crucify !

THE HIGH-PRIEST.

We bring this man to Pilate, charged with sin
Against the State.

CORNELIUS.

I'll take the man within.
But, Titus, hearken ; keep a watch the while ;
And should the crowd adventure force or guile,
Disperse them suddenly, and spare them not.

BOAZ.

The soldiers talk. Beware. A plot ! A plot !
Remember Pilate's murder of the men
Before his judgment-seat. Be careful then,
Or they will murder us. These, soldiers ? Nay,
But cowards, rogues, assassins. Don't delay
To set on us. Centurion, move on ; faster ;
And take this villain to your villain master.

(Three blasts of silver trumpets in the Temple hard by.)

THE LEVITES, *singing in the Temple.*

The Lord, our God, ascends his throne ;
For he shall reign and he alone.

He wears a vesture, pure and bright ;
And girds himself with power and might.

The land stands firm from shore to shore ;
Nor shakes again for evermore.

Thy throne has stood from olden days;
And ancient times unfold thy praise.

(Three blasts on the trumpets.)

THE CROWD, *to Pilate, as he enters.*

Away with the liar who seeks to remove
The customs and laws which the fathers approve.

THE PRIESTS.

He claims to be king of the Jews, and of late
Renewed the disorder which threatened the State.

PILATE.

Then take him hence, and judge him by your law.

ANNAS.

Your law forbids us put a man to death.

THE PRIESTS, *to Pilate, as he goes in.*

Let him be crucified. We never saw
A wretch who less deserved to draw a breath.

THE CROWD.

Away with him! The cross; for he must die!
Away, and crucify him! Crucify!

THE LEVITES, *singing in the Temple.*

The streams, O Lord, lift up their rebel waves:
The raging flood in madness roars and raves.

But thou art stronger than the breakers' roar:
Then bid the furious waves to rage no more.

(Three blasts on the trumpets.)

JOHN, *singing as he enters.*

    I am the World-child,
    Nursed by the sunshine,
    Cradled in visions,
    Robed in the splendours
    Flung by the storm-winds,
    Feeling the heart-beats,
    Throbbings and birth-throes,
    Pangs of my Mother.

BOAZ.

Here the mad poet comes. We'll place him there
As judge, upon the Roman's judgment-chair.

(As they seize him, he stands as in a dream, and pointing to the sky, speaks.)

JOHN.

Dark and Dawn would wed the World
Waking from her winter sleep,
And the Dark has almost hurled
Dawn within the dateless deep.

Pallid palls, which hoary Faith
Wove to hide her feeble arms,
Deck the Dark, and vanquish scathe
By the power of ancient charms.

Living lies and dead truths meet
On his brows, and twine, and kiss;
While beneath his miry feet
Yawns the gloom of Death's abyss.

Indistinctness weaves a shroud
For the Dawn, and veils his form
Trembling like a summer-cloud
In the passing of a storm.

BOAZ.

Now, fool, what else hast thou to tell to-day?

JOHN.

Nay; come, attend to what my lark will say.

ANNAS, SON OF ANNAS.

Be quiet, fool.

ALEXANDER.

We've had enough. Now cease.

BOAZ.

Nay, fool, go on. He'll keep the crowd in peace.

JOHN, *to his lark.*

Come, dear heart, forgive their scorning;
Sing once more for me this morning;
 Then I'll set thee free.
Silence; stand in quiet round me

Let no riot now confound me,
  While it speaks to me.

In early spring
I love to sing
Of earth and its robe of flowers,
  Of lilies, bright
  In morning light,
And blossoms on myrtle bowers.

  I wing my flight
  Till, out of sight,
My song is the voice of the sky ;
  But make my nest
  On earth's sad breast
To suffer with mortals who sigh.

  And minds in grief
  Will find relief,
For he, who will listen, still hears
  The notes of song,
  Both sweet and strong,
Till eye-stars will glisten with tears.

  I cheer the sad,
  And soothe the mad,
And waken the bad to noble strife ;
  So set me free,
  And I shall be
The herald of high and holy life.

TITUS.

Be off, thou fool, or I will seize thee.

JOHN.

But spare my lark ; it sings to please thee.

THE CROWD, *to Pilate entering with Jesus.*

Away with him, and let his life and name
Be never mentioned save as sign of shame.

THE LEVITES, *singing in the Temple.*

Thy word and work shall stand, established, fixed and sure ;
And holy beauty crowns thy House, while days endure.

(Three blasts on the trumpets.)

PILATE.

I find no fault in him.

ANNAS.

He is a vile
And evil-tongued deceiver. By his guile
He seeks to stir the people to rebel;
And now their rage is roused and bosoms swell.
He wanders through the land, and we can trace
His path from rebel districts to this place
By plots and murmurings and open threats,
For these are all his rebel speech begets.
He claims to be a king, and dares malign
Great Cæsar's honour and our sacred shrine.

PILATE.

Dost thou not hear how many charges lie
Against thee?

THE CROWD.

Crucify him; let him die!
Away; and crucify him! Crucify!

PILATE, *to Cornelius.*

Quick! bring Barabbas here to me.

(To the people.)
Ye brought
This man as one who wrought some crime and sought
To work deception and your nation's fall;
But see, I find in him no fault at all.

THE CROWD.

The cross! The cross! Away; and let him die!
Away; and crucify him! Crucify!

THE HIGH-PRIEST.

That wretch Barabbas comes. It is a choice.
Our friends must shout "Barabbas" with one voice.

PILATE.

Which of the two shall I free for you, choose
Either this rebel or him ye accuse.

THE CROWD.

Barabbas!   Barabbas!

PILATE.

Then what will ye choose
For him whom ye titled the King of the Jews.

THE CROWD.

The cross! The cross! Away; and let him die!
Away; and crucify him! Crucify!

PILATE.

But why? what evil has he wrought?
Or what sedition has he taught?

THE CROWD.

The cross! The cross! Away; and let him die!
Away; and crucify him! Crucify!

PILATE, *to Cornelius.*

Release that scoundrel. Take that man within,
And scourge him.

THE PRIESTS.

Hasten, Pilate; quick; begin
The work of God, and cause this fellow feel
What neither God nor man will help to heal.

BOAZ.

Be quick, thou butcher, Pilate; quickly go,
And send him to the place which soon shall know
Both thee and him; for, in the depths of hell,
Thy tyrant soul and he shall ever dwell.

ANNAS, *to the High-priest.*

They've gone within. 'Tis well. This day shall free
The State from many dangers. It shall be
The dawn of peace restored.

ALEXANDER, *to Annas.*

Thy speech was great
And strong in noble wrath. How Pilate quailed
Beneath thy eloquence! I said of late
To friends, Mark Annas now; he never failed.

ANNAS.

Thou art most kind. My humble efforts still
Fall short, nor reach the level of my will.

JOSEPH.

Nay; thou hast done so well that men unborn
Shall hail that man with praise and thee with scorn;
For, though the crowd may follow thee to-day,
They worship martyred men, and own their sway.

ALEXANDER, to *Annas.*

Nay; heed him not; his mind is warped, and cleaves
To every thought his fantasy conceives.

BARABBAS, to *Annas.*

I thank you, sir, although you were my foe,
For helping me this day. I do not know
The way to tell my thanks. I once could speak
And move the hearts of men; but sudden change
Of fortune seems to hold me dazed and weak,
As one who sees a vision passing strange.

ANNAS.

Yes; thou, no doubt, art grateful, and would'st shew
Thy gratitude. Then try, henceforth, to live
A better life, more honest, peaceful; so
Thy friends shall feel no shame, and thou shalt give
Us cause for joy in having rescued thee.

BOAZ.

Now, come; move on, Barabbas! I can't see.

ANNAS, SON OF ANNAS, to *Alexander.*

Go, find that poet somewhere in the crowd.
The noise and din are growing far too loud,
And soon we'll have a riot. There he stands.

ALEXANDER.

Come, madman, to the chair! Mankind demands
Thy sober judgment and thy wise decree.
Nay; seat thyself, nor seek to strive with me.

JOHN.

Well, hear the dream I dreamt this morn,
Which, like a vision, seemed to warn
My soul of ills that swell and surge
Around the world. What's that? A scourge!

BOAZ.

And thou shalt feel it soon.

ALEXANDER.

Come, quick. Dost hear?
The dream. The dream. Are we to wait a year?

JOHN.

I see the soul of darkest night
Enwrapt in robes of black and blight;
And, o'er the throne of all the world,
His banner floats in pride, unfurled.

A few stray locks of withered gray
About his wrinkled forehead play;
But from his eyes a ruddy blaze
Emits its fierce and scorching rays.

His thin and nervous fingers hold
A pen and parchment, worn and old;
His arm, of knotted sinews, shakes
As if his fearful spirit quakes;
While wags his beard as keeping time
To this, his wild and frantic rhyme:

" To me the lives of men are given
That they, o'erawed and terror-driven,
May seek beneath my Temple-dome
The stricken spirit's prison-home.

" For mine the sword to slay the soul
Which will not bow to my control:
In wrath, I drive it from the earth
To find in hell its second birth.

" And when deceived deceivers rose
Against my power, and would oppose
My word which is the word of God,
They perished at my angry nod."

But, while the spirit speaks, a ray
Of golden light announces day;
And all the eastern glories rise
And fling their radiance o'er the skies.

Behold, the glow and warmth invest
A woman, bearing at her breast
A babe which lies in sleep nor hears
The sound of mirth or falling tears.

The vision seems to grow and fill
The morning sky, now calm and still,
For worlds in silence stand and wait
In trembling hope the voice of fate.

And, while the Darkness strives to veil
The vision, while its clouds assail
The hosts of light, a whispered word
By all the world is plainly heard:

" The soul of future ages sleeps
While daylight o'er its features creeps;
And see, the Present now, at last,
Prevails to oust the cruel Past,
That so love's victories may shed
A glory round its infant's head."

BOAZ.

Enough! Enough! Be silent, fool; for look,
The governor returns.

ALEXANDER.

A jest! They took
That liar's clothes and robed him like a king.
Right regally the scarlet glories cling
About his shoulders. See the Roman wreath!
For sceptre, in his hands he bears a reed.

BOAZ.

That crown is made of thorns; for underneath
Its leaves the dreamer's head and temples bleed.

PILATE.

Behold the man!

THE PRIESTS.

Away; to die! To die!
Away; and crucify him! Crucify!

THE CROWD.

Away with him! Away! To die! To die!
Away; and crucify him! Crucify!

PILATE.

Behold your king!

THE CROWD.

Away with him! To die!
Away; and crucify him! Crucify!

PILATE.

What! Crucify your king?

THE CROWD.

Aye, crucify!

THE PRIESTS.

No king! He is no king of ours. We own
No king but Cæsar.

PILATE.

If the man must die
The crime of slaying him be yours alone,
For I am guiltless of his death; and, see,
I cleanse my hands and wash away the trace
Of blood. Then see to it.

THE PRIESTS.

His blood shall be
Upon our heads and on the Jewish race.

THE CROWD.

Away with him! Away! To die! To die!
Away; and crucify him! Crucify!

SCENE 9.—Calvary, facing the South.

(THE mound of Calvary is bleak and bare ;
   And scattered stones and heaps of rubble lend
   The scene those ruined aspects which offend
The sight already tortured by the glare.

And towards the south the city lies foursquare ;
   The walls and roofs and strong-built towers ascend
   The rising hills, and in their greyness blend
With clouds which hover in the azure air.

The sun, which shines on Olivet, is now
   Like one who passes from the early days
Of youth and life's first quarter, on whose brow
   Is seen no more the rare and radiant rays
Of innocence ; but newer powers endow
   With strength of soul no mortal may amaze.)

       BARUK, *alone*.
How strange that nature often seems
   A mirror for our feeling ;
And all the world a book of dreams
   Our inmost thoughts revealing.

And so this scene which I have known
   To waken wild ambition,
Where memory endows each stone
   With treasures of tradition,

Where Zion's proud and royal state,
   The Temple's golden glory,
Aroused the soul to emulate
   The brave of Jewish story ;

At other times has seemed to tell
    A tale of tearful sighing,
Of mournful crimes and woes which fell
    Upon the nation dying.

And now the scene appears to wear
    The robes of sullen frowning,
As if it spoke of grim despair
    And hopes in darkness drowning.

    HANNAH, *entering*.

I have come myself, conveying
    News which trembles on my lips :
Haste away, without delaying ;
    God but stays our lives' eclipse.

Scarcely had I made a mention
    Of thy name and hinted how
We had formed a firm intention,
    When his anger veiled his brow.

And my father said he's hiring
    Men to mark and murder thee ;
This he plans with hate untiring ;
    All thy crime thy love for me.

    BARUK.

Let me go, and, in some distant land,
    Toil in weariness for daily bread ;
While my soul, like Rizpah, takes her stand
    By her hopes, once cherished, but now dead,
To drive away the evil thoughts which prey
On noble dreams and cause their swift decay.

Yes ; I'll sail to Rome, and haply find,
    Spite of the scorn in which she holds the Jew,
Room to live in liberty of mind,
    Quickening the thoughts which law and custom slew ;
Yet there, as here, informers bear their tale
To those who rule ; and lies alone prevail.

    HANNAH.

Then go, and may thy life-star shine
    With glories never meant for me ;
If there be joys that may be mine,
    Let God transfer them all to thee.

And when, perchance, another maid
  Usurps my place within thy heart,
Shall then the once-loved image fade,
  And must thy love for me depart?

Or, when thy life is re-illumed
  With hope, and fortune sets thee high,
Wilt pity me whom God has doomed
  For love of thee to pine and die?

BARUK.

Not all the wealth the world possesses,
  Nor all that fancy dreams of fame,
Could dull the thought of thy caresses,
  Or dim the memory of thy name.

But would'st thou dare to trust me wholly,
  Forsake thy home, its joy and pride,
And face the world, dependent solely
  On my protection yet untried?

HANNAH.

  Yes; I'll confide in thee,
    Needing no guerdon
  But to abide with thee,
    Sharing thy burden.

BARUK.

  Sweetheart, life has no pang
    Piercing as love's distress
  When fate's venomous fang
    Poisons its happiness.

  Idly hope would declare
    Birth of the day from gloom,
  While faith's frenzied despair
    Garnishes passion's tomb.

  Action, mind of resource,
    Skill be our pilots now;
  Through the storm be our course;
    Darkness on poop and prow.

HANNAH.

Kiss me, dearest, with lips that cling
    Clasping the lips they love,
While our throats are a-throb and sing
    Songs of the rose and dove.

Kiss me, kiss me as once you kissed,
    Madly with heart on fire,
When the fury of passion hissed,
    Fervent with fierce desire.

Kiss me, holding me fast in arms
    Nerveless with wild delight,
Now while heaven attains new charms
    Seen as your satellite.

Kiss me, sovran of worlds of bliss,
    Now as your features fade,
Veiled in vapours which love like this
    Makes of a world unmade.

BARUK.

We need not seek far-distant lands,
    Or cross to Rome:
In Egypt yet a temple stands
    Amid a Jewish nation,
Where thought and speculation
    Have found a home.

And there our dreams will come again
    Thy dreams of love
As sweet as music's softest strain,
    My dreams of truth supernal;
    Till dreams become eternal
    In God above.

HANNAH.

'Tis so the Spirit of the world, who drapes
    Himself in human lives,
Unites the dreams of truth and love, and shapes
    The beauty which survives.

BARUK.

I had heard that God dwelt in each man,
    But believed that the tale was a lie,
Till my soul gathered courage to scan
    His flashing in flame from your eye.

And I feel that he fashioned your form
    For his fairest and holiest shrine,
Though he blast with the breath of the storm
    And the lightning his altar in mine.

    JUDAS, *entering and meditating*.

A God, who lived, had stayed my hand,
    Nor suffered him to be betrayed
Because I could not understand
    The vision which his speech displayed,
And raged to find the schemes I planned,
    Through what I counted dreams delayed.

    (He sees a flower at his feet.)

Ah, little floweret, whose love is arraying
    Thy bosom with beauty no man may attain?
Sweetly thou smilest while humbly displaying
    The ornaments wrought by the sun and the rain.

Art thou an angel, thus lowly disguising
    Thy glory and veiling thy beautiful face,
Come from the throne of the Highest, surprising
    The world with a vision of pureness and grace?

See, little floweret, I'll pluck thee as token
    Of light that again shall revisit my sky.
What have I done to thee? Lo, thou art broken,
    And now thou must languish and wither and die.

    BARUK, *to Judas*.

    Stranger, see you yonder throng?
    Is that Jesus dragged along?

    JUDAS.

Jesus! 'Tis he. 'Tis he; and where can I flee?
Vengeance of God! He follows me; follows me!
    (He goes out.)

HANNAH.

Slowly, slowly, comes the sad procession,
    Moving on its mournful road :
Sadly, sadly, bowed in deep depression,
    Jesus totters 'neath his load.

Bound as he, and like him bearing
    Boards to frame a bed of death,
Two men come, whose hearts despairing
    Tremble in their quick-drawn breath.

Roman soldiers, more unfeeling
    Than the soul in savage breast,
Deaf as stone to all appealing,
    Drive them on with scourge and jest.

Women follow from the city,
    Drawn by sympathy with woe,
Woe which rends the heart with pity,
    Pity such as women know.

BARUK.

But see, they strike him, fallen in a trance.
    The soldiers seize a passer-by, and bind
The beams on him. Once more the crowds advance ;
    And some with rage, and some with tears are blind.

HANNAH.

Why do such men, though scorned and hissed,
    Uplift the brow, as if the light
Of nobler worlds had crowned and kissed
    Them passing into death and night ?

BARUK.

For so the lightning wreathes in fire
The topmost branch and highest spire :
The fiercest forces flame in eyes
Which most prevail to cleave the skies,
Whose meteor-flashes gather strength,
    Illume their brow, consume their breast,
Until their passion proves at length
    To be a splendour and a pest.

HANNAH.

One hope, at times a feeble hope, has burned
   Within my heart, and I have ever nursed
   Its flame with dreams like those the seers rehearsed,
And for the day of higher manhood yearned.

But when a nobler spirit is discerned
   By other men, the meanest and the worst,
   His name is banned, his faith and fame aspersed,
And he himself with wrong and insult spurned.

BARUK.

For thus the good and great must ever tread
   The hero's path of stern self-sacrifice,
And with the legions of the famous dead
   They save the world from bonds of selfish vice;
O'er death in life their life in death will shed
   In death and life the love beyond all price.

JOHN, *to the Women.*

Weep not for him, nor pity his sorrow;
   Wail for the children ye cherish and love,
For ye will see a vengeance to-morrow,
   Such as the Highest ne'er hurled from above.

If this is done, Jerusalem's daughters,
   Unto the righteous, compared to the trees
Planted in strength by streams of the waters,
   What shall be done to the wicked at ease?

HANNAH.

O my God, I would shield him and shelter
   His form with my form; but I stay
Lest they beat me till wounded I welter
   Where blood of him blackens the clay.

BARUK.

He loses himself; but hereafter
   The world shall be won by the deed,
When death is forgotten in laughter
   And piety sanctifies greed.

But we have abandoned the worthless
   And wearisome world that we may
Obtain for us, wealthless and mirthless,
   Possession of self for a day.

HANNAH.

But this man lived to loosen earth
   From tyranny of hell,
To cause by word and deed the birth
   Of freedom's mighty spell.

And all who ever sought the same
   Have met a fearful fate,
For, driven from the earth in shame,
   They died 'mid yells of hate.

It seems that men are mad indeed,
   Nor recognise the soul
Which lives, and lives alone, to lead
   Their manhood to its goal.

BARUK.

Blind are the people ; the sin is not theirs ;
   They are untaught, and unable to know
Truth in its passion or love when it wears
   Vesture of poverty, weakness and woe.

Taught to admire the estate of the proud,
   Used from their childhood to follow the rich,
How can we blame them, an ignorant crowd,
   Born in a hovel to die in a ditch ?

Right is their heart, and hereafter it wakes,
   Wrathful with those who have led it astray,
Wakes to the sense of oppression, and breaks
   Bonds which the crafty have forged for their prey.

HANNAH.

See, he but tastes and refuses the cup which our ladies provide,
Soothing the pain of the hapless ; and see, as he puts it aside,
Fearless his face, and he stands in his patience, unmoved and alone
Gentle and calm, like a king on the day he ascends to his throne.

BARUK.

All the world is his who scorns
What it holds of good or ill,
Scorns its laurels and its thorns,
Strong in virtue, firm in will.

HANNAH.

Now the soldiers have unbound him,
  Standing king-like, though uncrowned ;
Now they gather close around him ;
  Now they fling him to the ground.
God of pity, does thy power avail ?
See, one takes the hammer and the nail.

CHILDREN OF NAZARETH, *entering and singing*.

Under our feet
  The flowerets are springing :
Voices as sweet
  As heaven are singing.

Coming is death ;
  The flowerets are dying ;
Songs, by his breath,
  Will change into sighing.

BARUK.

O God, where is thy power
In this woe-stricken hour
To stay these sinners from a deed mankind shall rue ?
  Oh, let thy curses fall ;
  In wrath consume them all.

JESUS.

Forgive them, Father, for they know not what they do.

SCENE 10.—A Meditation.

Calvary, looking towards the North.

(FLOODED with noontide flame, the scene grows vivid ;
    And on the skull-shaped mound the scorching glare
Beats fierce, and bathes pale forms and features livid,
    Whose death-sweat steeps their brows and tangled hair.

Nailed to their crosses, three men are suspended
    In spasms and unimaginable pangs,
Fathoming scorn no scorner comprehended ;
    And in the midst the Galilean hangs.

His eyes are swollen, nor perceive the glances
    Of curious men and women mad with woe ;
Nor see before them how the sunlight dances
    Until the city gleams with golden glow ;
And far behind him runs the northern road
To Nazareth, his happiest abode.)

THE WOMEN.

O Jesus, why must thou, so pure and gentle,
    Perish in pangs and leave us in despair ?
Is sin our sovran, and more elemental
    His force than hopes which happy love-dreams bear ?

Is God bereft of love to thee, his lover ?
    And will he watch while wickedness devours
The heart whose pain is potent to discover
    The latent power for wretchedness in ours ?

God's eyes are closed ; his lips forget the kisses
    By which his spirit mingled with thine own ;
His ears are deaf, nor heed the coward hisses
    Which mock the man who dared to stand alone.
O God, forgive our blasphemy, and save
Our best and bravest hero from the grave.

JOHN.

Disdaining death, my soul would prove an eagle
    Fearlessly hovering o'er the dark abyss ;
But thoughts arise, availing to inveigle
    My mind to moods of gloomy cowardice.

The consciousness of sin's unmeasured burden
    Trebles the grief which grows from actual wrong ;
And even now the everlasting guerdon
    Of sinfulness extinguishes my song.

What can I give to gain relief from Helldom
    Throned in my heart and darkening my days ?
Racked with corroding bonds, my life has seldom
    Leisure from self to offer prayer and praise.
O God, have mercy ; save me from despair
For sake of him who hangs in torture there.

BARUK.

Dark is the day, although the sun's at noon
    And smites the form of him who quivers, panting,
Filling the air with sorrows which attune
    The world to songs of dim, mysterious chanting.

And mists of tearful pity veil the skies
    Where dwells the Lord, beholding but unheeding
The myriad pangs in which his martyr dies
    And all the pathos of his silent pleading.

O God, thou hast dethroned thyself by this,
    And cruelly hast crowned this Man of Sorrow,
Whose spirit penetrates deep Hell's abyss
    To enter Heaven as thy God to-morrow ;
For Thought and Action fly from thee to vow
Allegiance to the peasant dying now.

JOSEPH.

So perishes the poor man known as herald
    Of juster ages speeding towards the earth ;
And even thus, in vain, the seers imperiled
    Themselves, their cause, and all they held of worth.

The polished worldling and the worldly pious
    Found here a foe who foiled their policy,
And, fortified by fear and party-bias,
    Suppress the voice of patient poverty.

And God, who clothes the morning in vermilion
    And vests the day-spring in green-azure pearled,
At noontide looks from his superb pavilion
    On misery the mantle of this world.
Ah, God, what portion have the poor in thee ?
For rich men's rods interpret thy decree.

BARUK.

Unhappy world, whose laughter pales this morning,
    For pity deifies self-sacrifice,
And pleasure fades before ascetic scorning
    Of Nature's virtue as a human vice.

The rich, red blood, which blackens in its streaming,
    Shall prove a symbol of our native fire
Grown dim to match the darkness of the dreaming
    In whose drear loneliness our loves expire.

Unhappy world, for whom the blood of martyrs
    Creates new blindness and a sterner reign
Than that which passes when its victim barters
    His life for fierce, unutterable pain ;
Since countless hearts must bleed to recompense
The patient woe of murdered innocence.

JOHN.

O Voice of God, at length I learn the meaning
    Of those deep words in which thy thoughts took form ;
And azure smiles through clouds of gloom careening
    O'er skies of terror in the spirit's storm.

Broken for me is passion's fiery phial
    From which I drank those fancies fugitive :
Give me instead the sternest self-denial,
    And let me drink of death that I may live.

Dead to the world in spiritual rapture,
    Deaf to its doctrines, curses and applause,
My spirit spurns its robe of flesh to capture
    A glimpse of God in his eternal laws;
And in that mystic world no sins molest
The peace which thou createst in the breast.

JOSEPH.

King of the Jews; for by that scornful title
    These men would move the multitude to mirth,
Unconscious that thy meekness claims requital
    Hereafter from the kingdoms of the earth.

Dimly aware, the world grows still with wonder,
    Scanning the words inscribed above thy head;
And lo, the robes of kings are rent asunder,
    Whose naked forms, like thine, are almost dead.

Now, in thy murder, kingship signs a sentence
    Of infamy against the royal name;
Nor can the law be changed by late repentance,
    For Nature's forces countersign the same.
Thus Tyranny expires in suicide,
And Meekness takes the throne usurped by Pride.

JOHN.

Meekest of men, remain to me as master,
    And live my lord, though slain in great disgrace;
For all the grief of infinite disaster
    Is weak to quench the godhead in thy face.

Within thy form, now palsied in death's rigour,
    Dwells an eternal virtue more divine
Than mortal man's, and potent to transfigure
    The frame it fashioned for its earthly shrine.

Beauty shall bring her brightest blooms to blazon
    The transient vision of a God revealed;
And Love shall chant through every diapason
    The fadeless love thy love of love shall yield;
For Death is slain at last in slaying thee,
And dies to seal thy deathless deity.

K

THE WOMEN.

Nothing more lovely has been ever given
    To woman's heart than thou in thy distress ;
And fired with seraph-love our souls are driven
    To mingle with thy soul in long caress.

And they whose lives are lone, unkissed, unwedded,
    Become thy brides in rapturous ecstasy,
Revelling in worship till their judgments credit
    Their passion's echo as a word from thee.

Led by thy love and spiritual beauty,
    Women accomplish thrice the work of men ;
Raising a cross to crown the road of duty,
    They brave all deaths in palace, camp, and den ;
Until the world shall pause from strife to learn
The mystic love with which our bosoms burn.

JOSEPH.

Weak are the slaves, and sluggish though affronted ;
    Many in number, but without a head.
What if their feelings, rude indeed and blunted,
    Instinctively should turn them to the dead ?

Then when thy failure is a scorn no longer,
    Marvel and mystery shall mould thy life
Until its force, transfigured, prove much stronger
    Than marshalled multitudes in freedom's strife.

We hope, perhaps, beyond what wisdom warrants,
    Dreaming of lands on some more sheltered shore ;
Yet we can act ; and deeds will swell the torrents
    Shattering custom in the breakers' roar ;
And when the barriers burst, the tides proclaim
Invincible the virtue of thy name.

BARUK.

Brave life, so loyal to the light of Heaven—
    If Heaven gave that light so pure and clear—
For good or evil, now thy words are leaven
    In human thought, and live till Time is sere.

But words like those thy gentle lips have uttered
    Are slain that their dead forms may serve as spell
To still the fears in which poor madmen muttered
    The incantations and the charms of Hell.

And in thy words of fiery indignation
    Another age may find an evidence
Supporting some despairing speculation
    To torture men with agonised suspense ;
Till God, supremely glorious in thy faith,
Shall seem to them a terrifying wraith.

JOHN.

Thy sweat and blood compose thy whole apparel ;
    But thou shalt wear God's glory on the morn
When thou returnest with triumphant carol
    To rule the men who murdered thee in scorn.

Millions shall mourn and cry to thee for mercy,
    Turning from idols which their lusts devised :
Silence succeeds ; for 'mid thy controversy
    The thunder's mute and lightning's paralysed.

But from the halo gleaming o'er thy forehead,
    And reminiscent of this thorny crown,
Terror, more dread than sin and hell are horrid,
    Shatters the world, and strikes its glories down.
Viewing the vengeance, all the universe
Shall laugh, relieved of this unmeasured curse.

BARUK.

Dear heart, what hast thou brought of love or loathing
    To gloom or gladden this frail life of ours ;
A fleeting hope ; or clinging hatred, clothing
    With irreligion man's convulsive hours ?

Though thou art mute and meek with seraph glory,
    Thy name outlives Jerusalem and Rome,
And rioting in vengeance, fierce and gory,
    Stains all the world a cruel monochrome.

For those who mocked thee in thy noon of sorrow
    Treble that mocking in thy noon of fame
When they're athirst for strife or power, and borrow
    Thy humble garb to sanctify their shame,
Surpassing Falsehood in the epigraph
Which they inscribe upon thy cenotaph.

JOSEPH.

The nets of shame which ancient Wrong has woven
    Dissolve before the murmur of thy name,
As all the clouds of Tyranny are cloven
    By Meekness, mighty in thy swordless fame.

A low-breathed whisper lulls the brutal quarrels
    Which cursed mankind with hate and hideous rage,
When Love, annihilating savage morals,
    Fulfils thy dreams, and brings the Golden Age.

Then Order wakens from the world's confusion;
    And Labour's laws set free the citizen,
Needing no aid from stupor and illusion
    To make its rule endurable by men;
For mortals, moved by faith, shall overwhelm
All helot states in one immortal realm.

THE WOMEN.

Thy soul and ours in mystical communion
    Shall multiply thy features, till the race
Bears the twin offspring of our wedded-union,
    Man's perfect grief and God's imperfect grace.

Then all whom love endows with love's acumen
    Shall recognise on every human brow
The symbol of a virtue more than human,
    But like to that which thou revealest now.

And we shall toil, though not unscorned or scathless,
    For thee thus mirrored in each human form
However frail it be, self-willed, or faithless,
    Or lightning-struck in earthly passions' storm,
That so the work of women may complete
The shrine of goodness built on thy defeat.

SCENE II.—A Dream.

The World of the Dead.

(In the land where no clouds ever hide
   The face of the far-off skies,
Where the tear-woven veil is untied,
   Which fell upon mortal eyes ;

In the wonderful world of the dead,
   The masters of men are seen
   With noble and lofty mien,
As if mirth and depression were fled.

   Their foeman, the lord of death,
   Deprived them of earthly breath,
But repaid them with all he could give,
For he gave them in dying to live.

And they live in that beautiful air,
Never troubled by sorrow or care,
   But dream, as they live in love,
   Of worthier worlds above.

   For love is a living scroll
In the letters and language of light,
And the more to the purified sight
   Its manifold texts unroll.

   At times, in their dreams, the rays
Of an earthlier light will appear,
   The light of the olden days,
Which is still to their memories dear.)

A GREEK BARD.

Ages and ages ago,
  When I sang but to pleasure the dying,
Clear were the voices, but low
  And distressful, which answered, replying:
" Why is applause for the brave
  Who are dead, with the people who followed?
Opened the jaws of the grave:
  Both the heroes and people were swallowed.
Sing not of battles, the joys
  And the pains of the men who have perished,
Themes which a woman employs
  In bewailing the son she has cherished.

" Sing of the living, dismayed,
  And the grief of the heart that is broken;
Sing of the darkness displayed
  By the chieftains of death as their token;
Sing of the struggle for life,
  And, attuning your accents to sorrow,
Wail o'er the wasting of strife
  And the gloom that is veiling the morrow."

Sterner and deeper the tones
  Of my heart as it wakened in anger:
" Turn from the weeping and groans,
  And resigning to women the languor,
Ever engage in the strife,
  As with strength of Immortals endowered;
Never the rage that is rife
  Can appal but the soul of a coward."

A KING OF BABYLON.

Across the clash of arms I heard
An echo of a nobler word,
Which never could have found its birth
Amid the mournful scenes of earth.
It flew from yonder flaming skies
To which it bade my soul arise
And, where the northern darkness shrouds
The peak of Elburz with the clouds,

To plant my feet, nor hesitate
To match Immortals with my state,
Beyond the starry circles climb,
And reign a god to endless time.

A HEBREW PROPHET.

The songs I sang were psalms of tears and shame :
For unto me the voice of sorrow came.

Thy tones set forth thy claim to reign with God :
I wept the captive race by thee down-trod.

Unknown to men, I sang the Servant's Song :
My nameless voice bewept my people's wrong.

They saw the star-light shine on Babel's stream :
But never hope's bright star on exiles' dream.

Can human mind such mournful mood conceive ?
Can human heart, unbroken, live to grieve ?

The nation, silent as a sheep, was slain :
And, lamb-like, died, nor murmured in its pain.

A voice announced for thee a lofty fate :
It echoed that which told their piteous state.

AN EASTERN MYSTIC.

Desires, conflicting, fill with woe
   The world of sense below :
Each gives his truest life to gain
Some fancied good through others' pain ;
And life, regarding life as foe,
   No rest can ever know.

But who can cause the strife to cease
And lead us to the perfect peace ?

Thus spoke the voice which, in my soul,
Was wont to warn me, and control :

" As the lily, when planted 'mid sights that offend,
   Shedding sweetness of beauty and fragrance around,
Is the righteous who dwells with the men who contend,
   For his life is with peace-giving peacefulness crowned.

"As the plant, when it flings off the flowers that have died,
   Is the righteous who casts all his self-love away,
And, divesting himself of his passion and pride,
   Lives to herald for mortals a happier day."

     But doubting still I asked again,
       Will then the righteous find release
     From all the bonds of earthly pain,
       And reach the life where sorrows cease?
     In dreamy tones the voice resumed
     The mournful tale of mortals doomed:

"When the body is lapped in the fire at the last,
   Then the soul, which was longing for rest from the strain
And the stress of its life, from its prison has passed
   To be born unto sorrow again and again."

     How wild the grief that filled my breast,
       And palsied every pulse and thought;
     For I would never reach that rest
       My soul had sorrowed for, and sought.

     The captive bird which spends its rage
       In foiled attempts to 'scape and fly,
     And with its wings would burst its cage,
       Has liberty at least to die.

     But, bound upon the rack of earth,
       The soul must view through endless years
     Its birth and death and still re-birth
       To sad inheritance of tears.

     And, trembling with despair, I said,
     Are life and grief for ever wed?
     Then, gently, like a whispered sigh,
     The voice of Buddha made reply:

"When boisterous winds no more with blasts disturb
   The fertile fields, the corn may stand in peace;
And when the passions, checked, are held with curb,
   The restless fevers of desire decrease;
For, while they rage, the heart can never cease
To mourn its dreams and fancies, unattained:
   Then slay desire, and so procure release
From life; and, lost to life, eternal rest is gained."

It seemed as when, amid a crowd,
　A strain of distant music steals,
Which, heard above the turmoil loud,
　A world of harmony reveals.
　　I sought the death in life which heals
Desire, and hastened to distil
　　The drug which lotus-death conceals
From all who boast a rebel will.

A WOMAN OF SHUNEM.

I would not ask one sorrow less,
　Of those which vexed my earthly years ;
I felt in them my God's caress,
　And heard his blessing in my fears.

When once a pleasure-loving king
　Commanded me to be his bride,
His ladies oft would softly sing
　In tones to wake my love and pride.

But they had torn me from my toil ;
　For mine it was to tend the field,
To guard from harm the vineyard's spoil,
　And watch the fruits the gardens yield.

They tore me from my lover's breast ;
　In vain they would my grief appease ;
And thus the singers I addressed,
　"Awake not love until it please."

For how could love endure to dwell
　Within such passing splendid halls,
Where only languid features tell
　Of those whom palling pleasure thralls ?

And, while the royal ladies sang
　As sweetly as my native rills,
My lover's voice still clearer rang
　On Lebanon's encedared hills.

" Come away, my little sweetheart, fly with me ;
　" For the winter is past,
　" And the summer at last
" In its beauty comes to greet the land and sea.

"Now the flowers are bearing robes to deck the earth;
"Birds are singing above;
"Doves are cooing of love;
"And the fruit-trees share the universal mirth."
But still I knew the dawn would break,
   And every shadow flee away,
When sleeping love at last would wake
   To live in love's eternal day.

HER LOVER.

Yes; my sweetheart, woman's truth and faith were thine;
   Truth, exceeding belief;
   Faith, that vanquishes grief
When its pure white light and youth's rose glow combine.

THE WOMAN OF SHUNEM.

And, when at length the king withdrew,
   I found within my lover's arms
   A home where never ills pursue
With vain regrets or wild alarms.

But all the light of later years,
   Which grew upon the growing sight,
   Became a rainbow's varied light
That sparkles in those early tears.

In grief, the joys of other days
Are seen through gloom and tearful haze:
In joy, remembered grief will wear
The semblance of an angel fair.

THE CHORUS OF THE DEAD.

Who comes to trouble this region so blest
   By a countenance heavy with woe,
Like one whose spirit might never have rest
   From the care and the struggle below?

JUDAS, *entering*.

Nay; touch me not, for crimes still stain
   My soul with guilty fears;
And wild remorse consumes my brain,
   Nor finds relief in tears:
The memories of sin remain
   To grieve through changeless years.

THE CHORUS OF THE DEAD.

Dark must the sin be,
Raging within thee,
O'er death prevailing,
Vengeance entailing.

Light now is growing
Brighter and glowing,
Radiant with splendour,
Gracious and tender.

Who is ascending,
Hitherward tending?
Vision possessing
Infinite blessing.

JESUS, *entering*.

I come from a planet below,
Whose sun in the distance afar
Is seen as an indistinct star ;
Where winds of remembrances blow
In sadness, and memories wave
Like cypresses over the grave
Of dreams that were brighter than day,
Of hopes that have vanished away ;
And there did I toil, for I willed
In storm-beaten bosoms to build
A kingdom, with peacefulness filled.

THE CHORUS OF THE DEAD.

Noble spirit, speak and say,
  Upon what throne did mortals place thee?
With what symbol of thy sway
  Did happy men delight to grace thee?

JESUS.

Behold my hands, my feet, my side.

THE CHORUS OF THE DEAD.

Ingrates ! Thou hast been crucified.
About thy head we bind the poet's crown,
For thine his thoughts, his grief, his great renown ;
The diadems of kings to thee belong,
For thou hast led the world to war with wrong ;

The priestly crown and mitre is thine own,
For thou hast found the sorrows which atone,
The progress gained by sacrifice alone.
Then reign a poet-priest upon thy throne;
And, with the triple crown upon thy head,
Be thou for ever monarch of the dead.
At length in rest and peace begin thy reign,
And here the purpose of thy life attain.

JUDAS.

Do not, Master, thus meet me, directing thy gaze
On the worm at thy feet with the glance of the days
That are fled; but with curses invoke every woe
On my head, and I'll turn from thy presence and go.

JESUS.

Friend, thy life was not in vain.
  When, illumined by thy grief,
Thou shalt rise and strive again,
  God will haste to thy relief.

Spirits, dream not yet of rest;
  There are worlds unknown, untrod;
Speed on hence with zeal and zest,
  Upwards to the throne of God.

THE CHORUS OF THE DEAD.

Thou, whom the holy
Light is adorning,
Aid us that, scorning
Base things and lowly,
We may see clearer
Goal of our dream,
Ever draw nearer
God the supreme.

JESUS.

The earth's own shadow makes the moon-light less,
  And veils from view that poor reflected beam:
Men shroud the truth with their own nothingness,
  And dim the light in man with their own dream.

Behold the light itself, no borrowed gleam ;
    Then strive to gain it, as, in dark distress
Ye passioned for it ; strive, till every stream
    Of light has led to God, who waits to bless.

Still onward, upward ; wake the noblest chord
    Of all the heart-strings ; ever yearn, aspire ;
Nor let some fading world eclipse the lord
    Of day, and shroud the source of truth and fire :
Still seek the noblest work and such reward
    As suits the hero-soul whom naught could tire.

THE CHORUS OF THE DEAD.

Nobly thou speakest,
Nerving the weakest
    Still to endeavour.
Skies, rent asunder,
Echo in thunder,
    " Upward for ever."

SCENE 12.—An After-thought.
Earth and Heaven.

O BRIDE of my dream-life, the songs of my chanting
   Are pale and appear unimpassioned and cold,
Compared with thy bosom's most rhythmical panting
   Beneath its apparel of purple and gold.

Through numberless years I have nursed the wild wonder
   Which longed to decipher the flame-written scroll
Encircling thy brow and to learn in the thunder
   The word that unveiled thee and uttered thy soul.

My will was bewitched by the worth of mine idol,
   But now I am nearing the foot of thy throne
To fling round thy spirit the spell of our bridal
   And fashion my faith as a star for thy zone.

HEAVEN.

I read upon each crag and cliff,
   Though vested in a robe of mist,
Thy secret veiled in hieroglyph;
   But, on the peaks my lips have kissed,
   The morning, like a melodist,
Tells of thy love and lonely tears
To all the suns in all the spheres
Until the whole creation hears.

Above thy rough and wrinkled face,
   Age has entwined a wreath of snows,
But in thy pulses finds no place
   For placid peace and calm repose,

Where passions throb in fiery throes
Born of primeval night's abysm
To lap thy life in shock and schism
And clothe thee with a cataclysm.

Though ruin rules thy realm as yet,
  In this thy hope is evidence
Of days to dawn, when fume and fret,
  Appeased by passion's recompense,
  Shall yield thy heart to love intense
Which even now awakes and strips
Away the cloud of thine eclipse
And proves thy soul's apocalypse.

EARTH.

I have trodden the anguish of poignant betrayal
  And faltered on verge of a loathsome abyss,
But the impulse which moved me to make the essayal
  Is crowned as divine by a moment like this.

All my dread, lest the beauty I dreamed was illusion
  Transforming the sepulchred horrors of death,
Is dispelled by the splendours in spendthrift profusion
  Bestowed on the stars by the waves of thy breath.

I would clasp thee and cling to thee, glad in those glances
  Which waken delight in my woodlands and streams,
For the thrill of affection is felt and entrances
  My heart with a rapture unknown to my dreams.

HEAVEN.

The grandeur of thy granite limbs
  Which tremble with their strong desires
Prevail beyond thy chain of hymns,
  Moulded on passion-broken lyres ;
  But neither woo me as the fires
Mantling in lustres vale and hill
Where Autumn's magic wands distil
The glories in the chlorophyll.

But dearer are those puny forms,
   Whom vehemence and madness rule
And make the playthings of the storms;
   For, scorning reason's ridicule,
   They build of verse a vestibule
To this great Temple, where I dwell
Throned on the deep whose tidal swell
Is mystery and miracle.

Yet not for these I love thee most,
   But for the men impelled to climb
Life's spiral pathway, unengrossed
   By fear of phantoms formed in slime,
   Who, having battled with their time,
Shall pass within my Temple-gate
And hear the ages celebrate
Their lives with love immaculate.

EARTH.

By remains of the mortals who moved thee to love me,
   By labours of heroes who hallowed my toil,
Let thy mercy which hovers for ever above me
   Look down on the grime of my soul, and assoil.

Oh, remember the men whom the multitude martyred
   And slew for allegiance to freedom and truth,
And have thought for the feeble who thoughtlessly bartered
   For pleasure the valorous impulse of youth.

Do thou yield to the wild inarticulate yearning
   In wails of the wind and in sobs of the sea,
For the rapture of ecstasy fills me discerning
   Supremest existence as mirrored in thee.

THE WELCOME BY SORROW.

Out of her lips leaped a song that was part of her,
   Broke into stars on the brow of the night,
Each of them winged with a dream from the heart of her,
   Bathed in her beauty and thrilled with delight.

Love-light sprang forth and was fain of repaying her,
   Flew to her bosom with flame which excels
Even the beauty of dreamland arraying her
   Dimly in music and magical spells.

Silence and darkness beheld and grew amorous,
   Kindling and fanning their fire with her breath
Till they were clothed as the noontide and clamorous,
   Bursting the bars of imprisoning death.

Ages arose from the grave-land of history,
   Hastened to robe her in garments of old,
Wrought of the beautiful pallor of mystery,
   Faintly suffused with impalpable gold.

All that the universe veiled was revealed to her,
   All of its treasures disclosed to her gaze;
All that was living and loving appealed to her,
   Yielding her worship and waiting her praise.

Then when eternity panted its passional,
   Fawned at her feet with the plaint of the sea,
Lo, she was moved by an impulse irrational,
   Spurned all the splendours and smiled upon me.

THE FAREWELL TO THE POEM.

Why dost thou weep, poor child, unless to be
A partner in thy parent's misery,
Whose early flames were flung on sterile ways
Where weariness had well-nigh quenched the blaze ;
And these my tears are shed because thy frame
Shakes with thy father's and his fathers' shame.

Save for thyself thy treasury of tears,
For soon the world prepares its rack and shears
To mar thy shape, and frets with fool and knave
Thy path from mother-breast to mother-grave,
Until the bane of birth and ills of life
Madden ; but madness multiplies the strife.

But leave me now, for faint and ill at ease,
I hear an elegy in every breeze
Which breathes thy name, but know not if the breath
Whispers of mine or thine approaching death ;
Yet I would live to make another song
To soothe my pain and half-redeem thy wrong.

www.ingramcontent.com/pod-product-compliance
Lightning Source LLC
Chambersburg PA
CBHW030259170426
43202CB00009B/810